Thomas Cook

CITYSPOTS
LEIPZIG

WHAT'S IN YOUR GUIDEBOOK?

Independent authors Impartial up-to-date information from our travel experts who meticulously source local knowledge.

Experience Thomas Cook's 165 years in the travel industry and guidebook publishing enriches every word with expertise you can trust.

Travel know-how Thomas Cook has thousands of staff working around the globe, all living and breathing travel.

Editors Travel-publishing professionals, pulling everything together to craft a perfect blend of words, pictures, maps and design.

You, the traveller We deliver a practical, no-nonsense approach to information, geared to how you really use it.

CITYSPOTS
LEIPZIG

Written by Kerry Walker
Updated by Cinnamon Nippard

Published by Thomas Cook Publishing
A division of Thomas Cook Tour Operations Limited
Company registration No: 1450464 England
The Thomas Cook Business Park, 9 Coningsby Road
Peterborough PE3 8SB, United Kingdom
Email: books@thomascook.com, Tel: +44 (0)1733 416477
www.thomascookpublishing.com

Produced by The Content Works Ltd
Aston Court, Kingsmead Business Park, Frederick Place
High Wycombe, Bucks HP11 1LA
www.thecontentworks.com

Series design based on an original concept by Studio 183 Limited

ISBN: 978-1-84848-045-2

First edition © 2007 Thomas Cook Publishing
This second edition © 2009 Thomas Cook Publishing
Text © Thomas Cook Publishing
Maps © Thomas Cook Publishing/PCGraphics (UK) Limited
Transport map © Communicarta Limited

Series Editor: Lucy Armstrong
Production/DTP: Steven Collins

Printed and bound in Spain by GraphyCems

Cover photography (Fountain Mendebrunnen at Augustusplatz) © imagebroker/Alamy

CONTENTS

CITYSPOTS

SYMBOLS KEY

The following symbols are used throughout this book:

ⓐ address ☎ telephone ⑤ fax ⓦ website address
🕐 opening times ⓝ public transport connections ❶ important

The following symbols are used on the maps:

𝒊 information office   ▪ points of interest
✈ airport   O city
✚ hospital   O large town
🛡 police station   o small town
🚏 bus station   = motorway
🚆 railway station   — main road
✝ cathedral   — minor road
❶ numbers denote featured   — railway
    cafés & restaurants

Hotels and restaurants are graded by approximate price as follows:
£ budget price **££** mid-range price **£££** expensive

⏵ *Old meets new in Leipzig's city centre*

INTRODUCING
Leipzig

Introduction

Saxony's Sleeping Beauty has awoken from its communist slumber and is staging its comeback as one of Europe's hottest cities. One-time home to such luminaries as Bach, Goethe and Wagner, Germany's eastern gem has returned to its cultural roots, showcasing cabaret in secluded courtyards and music in sublime concert halls. For classical music, art and comedy fans, the love affair with Leipzig begins here.

But with the tide of tradition come the waves of innovation. Bright-eyed and bushy-tailed, this 500,000-strong university city bubbles over with avant-garde architecture, funky cafés, modern malls and all-night parties. From caipirinhas by the canals in red-bricked Plagwitz to Michael Fischer-Art's multicoloured murals, Leipzig blends cultural clout with cutting edge. There's an undeniable whiff of energy and excitement in the air.

Leipzig wears its riches well: cobbled squares and Gothic spires, boutique-lined arcades and museums creaking under the weight of their treasures, never-ending parks and cavernous cellars are ripe for the picking. Whether you want to join the cheery locals for an alfresco coffee break, hear Bach's cantatas in St Thomas's Church or dance till dawn on Barfussgässchen, this is the place. Thanks to its being a relatively inexpensive city, Leipzig offers good times that don't result in an overdraft.

Stepping away from the centre, Gohlis beckons with its immaculate art nouveau townhouses, while Plagwitz revamps the industrial landscape with gondola rides on its tree-fringed waterways. Leipzig goes green in Rosental's peaceful heathland

and the Auenwald floodplain forest, making it easy to escape the city's throngs.

Linger longer to unravel Halle's clutch of baroque buildings and medieval castles strung along the River Saale. The UNESCO World Heritage Site of Dessau-Wörlitz Gartenreich sprouts manicured gardens and rococo palaces. Here you can revel in the splendour of royalty, bike through acres of greenery and be inspired by Bauhaus creations – all just a stone's throw away from Leipzig.

⬥ *Bach is one of the city's famous sons*

When to go

Leipzig is not a city of meteorological extremes (see below).
Spring is the time to enjoy Rosental Park and the Botanic
Gardens in bloom. Autumn is when culture hits its high, with
events such as the Laughter Fair and Jazz Days taking audiences
by storm. In winter you can explore Leipzig's illuminated
Christmas Market (see page 14), one of Germany's finest.

SEASONS & CLIMATE

The city has a moderate climate, with summers not too hot,
peaking at around 25°C (72°F) and winters not too cold; the
temperature rarely dips below 0°C (32°F). Spring temperatures
hover between 10°C and 15°C (48°F and 56°F). Leipzig basks in
sunshine from June to August, but also gets its fair share of rain,
so come prepared for sudden downpours. If you're planning on
hiking the Auenwald forest, autumn is a safe bet with mild,
dry days. Wrap up warm in winter.

ANNUAL EVENTS

March

Leipzig Book Fair Bury your head in books at Leipzig's
celebration of the written word. Expect readings, lectures
and debates at this important literary event. ⓐ Messe-Allee 1
ⓣ 0341 678 8240 ⓦ www.leipziger-buchmesse.de

April & May

A Cappella Festival Artists stretch their vocal chords at this musical
highlight, staging everything from polyphonic song to vocal jazz

in churches and concert halls across the city. ☎ 0341 910 2244
🌐 www.a-cappella-festival.de

⏶ *Relaxing in the balmy climate*

May

Pop-Up Festival Pan-genre pop fest with an emphasis on new bands and DJs. ☎ 0341 225 3400 ⓦ www.leipzig-popup.de

June

Bach Festival Leipzig pulls the stops out for this ten-day festival of orchestral highs, dedicated to the city's most famous past resident, the lad himself, Johann Sebastian Bach. ☎ 0341 913 7302 ⓦ www.bach-leipzig.de

Wave Gothic Meeting Leipzig reveals its darker side at this huge Gothic meeting, featuring open-air concerts, exhibitions, theatre and late-night parties. Dates jump around a bit, so check the website for details. ☎ 0341 212 0862 ⓦ www.wave-gotik-treffen.com

July

Saxonia International Balloon Fiesta Going up! Leipzig looks to the skies as hundreds of hot air balloons float above the city at this five-day summer festival. As well as a whole lotta hot air, there are fireworks and plenty of family attractions. ☎ 0341 868 050 ⓦ www.balloons.de

October

International Leipzig Festival for Documentary and Animated Film Cutting-edge documentaries, shorts and animation from across the globe draw film buffs to this week-long festival. ☎ 0341 308 640 ⓦ www.dok-leipzig.de

Laughter Fair Leipzig loves to laugh at this festival featuring the cream of the comedy crop. Giggle and guffaw at German and

international stand-up acts and cabaret. ❶ 0341 878 0570
🅦 www.lachmesse.de

November
**euro-scene Leipzig – Festival of Contemporary European
Theatre** All the world's a stage at this dramatic six-day festival,
hosting plays, premieres and improvised theatre in top venues.
❶ 0341 980 0284 🅦 www.euro-scene.de

December
Christmas Market Festive goodies make this one of Leipzig's
must-visit attractions (see pages 14–15).

PUBLIC HOLIDAYS
Neujahrstag (New Year's Day) 1 Jan
Heilige Drei Könige (Epiphany) 6 Jan
Karfreitag (Good Friday) 10 Apr 2009; 2 Apr 2010; 22 Apr 2011
Ostermontag (Easter Monday) 13 Apr 2009; 5 Apr 2010;
25 Apr 2011
Maifeiertag (Labour Day) 1 May
Christi Himmelfahrt (Ascension Day) May
Pfingstmontag (Whit Monday) May/June
Tag der deutschen Einheit (Day of Unity) 3 Oct
Reformationstag (Day of Reformation) 31 Oct
Buß- und Bettag (Repentance Day) Nov
Erster Weihnachtstag (Christmas Day) 25 Dec
Zweiter Weihnachtstag (Boxing Day) 26 Dec

Leipzig Christmas Market

Leipzig's month-long Christmas market breathes seasonal cheer into the centre, with Christmas trees and glowing fairy lights. Dating back to 1767, the market hums with carol singers, carousels and the world's largest freestanding advent calendar. Measuring a mammoth 857 sq m (9,225 sq ft), the super-sized calendar on Böttchergasse is one every child would love to have on their wall. Ensure you're there at 16.30 between 1 and 24 December to watch one of the huge doors being opened.

Even Scrooge would melt at the sight of the nativity scene on Augustusplatz, where a flock of real sheep are brought in for the occasion – bah humbug indeed! A focal point of the festivities, this square shrinks beneath a 20 m (66 ft) giant of a Christmas tree, bedecked in thousands of tiny lights. Kids are kept entertained, slipping and sliding across the open-air ice rink or visiting Father Christmas at the glittering winter wonderland complete with Finnish reindeer.

Feeling peckish? Little wonder with the Christmassy whiff of *Glühwein* (mulled wine) and fresh pretzels tempting on every corner. Taste sugary specialities such as *Pulsnitzer Pfefferkuchen* (chocolate-coated gingerbread) and *Leipziger Räbchen* (cinnamon doughnuts filled with plums and marzipan). All this may seem like an adventure in cholesterol, but who cares, it's Christmas!

If it is gifts you're after, there are more than 260 stalls encouraging you to loosen your purse strings. Look out for the hand-carved decorations, incense smokers, nativity pyramids, wooden crib figures and brightly coloured nutcrackers from the Erzgebirge mountains.

Musical highlights of this yuletide event include brass band concerts in front of the Opera House on Augustusplatz and the renowned Thomanerchor (St Thomas's Boys Choir), which has a history dating back nearly 800 years, performing at St Thomas's Church. To feel the true spirit of Christmas, take a peek at around 800 intricate nativity scenes on display in the Old Town Hall. The festivities culminate just before Christmas Eve with a spectacular parade and concert in the city centre. **Leipzig Tourist Service** ⓐ Richard-Wagner-Strasse 1 ⓣ 0341 710 4265 ⓦ www.leipzig.de ⓛ 09.30–18.00 Mon–Fri, 09.30–16.00 Sat, 09.30–15.00 Sun & public holidays, Mar–Oct; 10.00–18.00 Mon–Fri, Nov–Feb

🔺 *The world's biggest advent calendar dominates the Christmas Market*

History

A city with a turbulent past, Leipzig is now looking towards a brilliant future. With a strategic location between Eastern and Western Europe, the city has been marked by many changes and foreign influences over the ages, and has played a pivotal role in shaping the history of Saxony and Germany.

While Leipzig's roots stretch back as far as the 7th century, when Slavic settlers occupied the banks of the Elster and Parthe rivers, the city was first mentioned in writing in 1015 in the Bishop Thietmar von Merseburg's chronicle. In 1165, the city was granted 'market rights'; two trade fairs a year were held, sparking off a period of unparalleled growth which saw Leipzig become one of Europe's most important trade routes.

In 1409 the University of Leipzig was founded, and the city began to prosper and progress in both law and publishing. A key milestone was achieved in 1481 when Leipzig's first book was printed by Marcus Brandis, and in 1519 Leipzig became the focus of European attention when the leader of the Protestant Reformation, Martin Luther, denied the divine right of the pope in the dramatic Leipzig Debate. Leipzig accepted the Reformation in 1539.

The 17th century brought a mixture of tragedy and triumph for Leipzig. Battles fought at Breitenfeld and Lützen during the Thirty Years War (1618–48) left a trail of destruction and disease in their wake. Yet at the same time the city thrived as a centre of academic excellence. The world's first-ever newspaper was printed here in 1650 and the city was home to gifted men such as philosopher and mathematician Gottfried Wilhelm von

Leibnitz and composer Johann Sebastian Bach, cantor at
St Thomas's Church from 1723 until his death.

The University of Leipzig reached its literary peak in the
18th century, shining with illustrious scholars such as Schiller,
Gellert and Goethe, who studied law from the age of 16 and
wrote many of his early plays and poems in the city. The
Auerbachs Keller restaurant is mentioned in his drama *Faust*.

In 1813, Prussian forces defeated Napoleon's troops at the
Battle of Leipzig. The Monument to the Battle of the Nations
commemorates the many thousands that lost their lives in the
battle. On a more positive note, Leipzig gave rise to some of the
world's greatest composers in the 19th century, including Felix
Mendelssohn, Robert Schumann and Richard Wagner, who
established musical academies and concert halls such as the
Leipzig Conservatory and Gewandhaus.

A spurt of growth in the early 20th century was brought
to a sudden halt with the advent of World War II (1939–45):
thousands of Jewish residents were killed and much of the city
was reduced to rubble in the 1943 bombings. After the war,
unrest bubbled under the city's surface until in 1989 Leipzig's
Monday demonstrations evolved into the biggest protest ever
against the East German regime, ultimately leading to the
downfall of the communist government and German
reunification in 1990.

The city is looking good, thanks to an economic boom fuelled
by the opening of the Porsche and BMW manufacturing plants.
The 2006 FIFA World Cup was a real profile-elevator, and Leipzig
has over the past decade become one of Germany's most
exciting cities.

Lifestyle

The only way is up for Leipzig. With its futuristic trade fair, glittering malls and revolutionary art centres, it's hard to believe this city was caught in the clutches of communism just two decades ago. Today, Leipzig has risen like a phoenix from the communist ashes and is growing leaps and bounds in culture, industry and business. Tie that with the kick it got out of the FIFA World Cup 2006, a resounding success, and you are looking at a city that feels confident and comfortable in its own skin.

And it shows. A glance at the Leipzig locals confirms they are an easy-going and down-to-earth bunch who know how to enjoy themselves. They make no secret of their passion for music – which you'll hear on every street corner; art in every shape and form; partying (as a blurry-eyed night out on Barfussgässchen will confirm), and sport – football and athletics to be exact. Strike up a conversation on any one of these topics and you're bound to get a good response. Most inhabitants speak English, but test out your German if you want to impress.

Buzzing and free-spirited, Leipzig's 16,700 students give the city a forward-looking, multicultural feel that is welcoming to travellers. While its baroque, Renaissance and art nouveau architecture may scream 'traditional', this liberal city has a rebellious streak and a passion for the peculiar. It's impossible not to feel relaxed in a place where Goths and lawyers chew the cud over coffee, or punks and academics philosophise over a glass of gold-hued *Gose* beer. A melting pot of cultures and subcultures, this is one place where you really can come exactly as you are.

CHILDREN OF THE REVOLUTION

Daring and defiant, Leipzig has never been afraid to stand up for what it believes in. Nikolaikirche was at the centre of the peaceful Monday demonstrations in 1989, where thousands flocked to pray for peace. The movement spread to other German cities, culminating in the events of 9 October 1989, when 70,000 people took to the streets to demonstrate against the communist regime, with the famous chant *Wir sind das Volk* ('we are the people'). Just a month later, the Berlin Wall came down and paved the way for German reunification.

⬤ *Music forms a backbeat to this exciting city*

Culture

Leipzig doesn't just display its culture behind glass: it lives and breathes it. Having been home to Bach, Wagner and Mendelssohn, it's little wonder music and art run through this city's veins. Leipzig supports the underdog, too, making waves with innovative and inspiring art forms. From free violin concertos on Thomaskirchhof to Michael Fischer-Art's astonishing open-air creations, this is one city where you don't have to spend money to enjoy cultural delights.

Leipzig's acclaimed orchestra performs in the frescoed Gewandhaus on Augustusplatz (see page 66). Across the square is the Opera House (see page 66), for opera, musicals and ballet. At weekends, Thomaskirche (see page 65) resonates to the warbling of famous choirs.

Visitors who enjoy a laugh and understand a little German should catch one of Leipzig's superb cabaret and variety shows. At the forefront of satirical and stand-up comedy, venues such as Academixer (see page 65) stage regular performances in centuries-old buildings and courtyards. For the linguistically challenged, **Krystallpalast Variete** (ⓐ Magazingasse 4 ❶ 0341 140 660 ⓦ www.krystallpalast.de) offers an eclectic programme featuring everything from contortionists to gravity-defying trapeze artists.

Improvised art and jam sessions are at their best in the underground vaults of the red-brick Moritzbastei (see page 76), a popular student haunt set around a central courtyard. When it comes to graphic art, Leipzig has its own superstar, Neo Rauch, the most famous member of the New Leipzig School, a movement that idealises life in the city before the Communists took over.

⬤ *The opera house is part of a vibrant cultural scene*

THE DARLING OF DARING ART

Walking around Leipzig, you can't fail to notice Michael Fischer-Art's in-your-face colours and larger-than-life characters, often splashed against the sides of public buildings. The Leipzig-born artist is not shy when it comes to wielding his paintbrush to create bold and bright designs that are magnets to contemporary art lovers. Opposite the Fine Arts Museum, his surreal murals have given new life to the Drei Türme, three derelict concrete tower blocks on Brühl, which are now quite a shock to the senses!

If you like your art raw and edgy, venture further south to check out the offerings at Werk II (see page 85), a revamped factory churning out alternative plays, concerts and films. Another offbeat one to watch out for is naTo (see page 84), hosting wacky events alongside jazz sessions, art house films and modern dance productions.

The glass-walled MDBK (Museum of Fine Arts, see page 66) houses German Expressionism – glimpse Max Klinger's *Beethoven* – plus Dutch Masters and Impressionist works by artists such as Rodin. More modern pieces grace the walls of the Contemporary Art Gallery (see page 84) and the maze-like Baumwollspinnerei (see page 83), housed in a former cotton mill. To be literally surrounded by art, check out Yadegar Asisi's striking 360° panoramas in the Asisi Factory Panometer (see page 78) – certain to raise eyebrows.

⏵ *Markt – Market Square – forms the hub of Leipzig*

Shopping

From original boutiques to art deco antiques, Leipzig keeps shoppers on their toes. Dip into the city centre's pockets to uncover high-street stores and glass-walled malls, old-world arcades and markets with mountains of seasonal produce.

Shops are open six days a week. Opening hours are generally 10.00–19.00 Monday to Friday and 10.00–16.00 Saturday, although major shopping malls like the Promenaden Hauptbahnhof at Leipzig's main station (see page 70) stay open daily until 22.00.

Fashionistas seeking the latest styles make for Petersstrasse, Grimmaische Strasse and Neumarkt, where department store giant Galeria Kaufhof (see page 69) is an enjoyable one-stop shop. Unique gifts such as wooden Erzgebirge decorations and Meissener porcelain fill the speciality shops that huddle around Markt and Naschmarkt. Eagle-eyed collectors sniff out antiques and second-hand books in Katharinenstrasse.

Leipzig is punctuated with elegant arcades. Topping the list is the partly-Renaissance, partly-art nouveau Mädler Passage (see page 69), which houses big-name smart boutiques. With its frescoes and hidden courtyards, the elegant Specks Hof arcade (see page 70) is the perfect place to pick up fine wines and original art.

You'll find 140 shops, restaurants and cafés beneath the Promenaden Hauptbahnhof's glass roof (see page 70). Big names like Mango, Yves Rocher, Swatch and Esprit cluster here, plus souvenir shops, bookshops and a handful of designer boutiques. Pick up funky footwear and sweet treats in the ultra-modern Petersbogen mall opposite the town hall (see page 70).

Leipzig has plenty of markets. Stalls are piled high with fresh produce every Tuesday and Friday at Leipzig's fresh food market (ⓐ Markt Platz 1 🕐 09.00–17.00). Find bric-à-brac at the flea market (ⓐ Alte Messe) on the first weekend of the month and hidden gems at the antique market (ⓐ Agra Park, Bornaische Strasse 210) on the last. Buy blooms at May's flower market,

⬥ *Relaxed retail therapy in the Mädler Passage*

USEFUL SHOPPING PHRASES

What time do the shops open/close?
Um wieviel Uhr öffnen/schließen die Geschäfte?
Oom veefeel oor erffnen/shleessen dee geshefter?

How much is this?
Wieviel kostet das?
Veefeel kostet das?

Can I try this on?
Kann ich das anprobieren?
Can ikh das anprobeeren?

My size is ...
Ich habe Größe ...
Ikh haber grerser ...

I'll take this one, thank you
Ich nehme das, danke schön
Ikh neymer das, danker shern

This is too large/too small/too expensive
Es ist zu groß/zu klein/zu teuer
Es ist tsu gross/tsu kline/tsu toyer

local brews at July's Beer Exchange, or hand-carved decorations and gingerbread at December's Christmas market (see page 14).

For a lingering taste of Leipzig, take home some delicious, cream-filled *Bachpfeiffen* chocolates from Arko in the Mädler Passage and coin-shaped *Bachtaler* pralines from Café Kandler (see page 71).

Wrap and pack delicate Meissen porcelain, *Gose* beer (and the glass to match), and hand-carved Christmas decorations from Heidrich & Zeidler.

Eating & drinking

Both the food and the prices are appetising in Leipzig, whipping up traditional, world and new-wave flavours. Go underground to savour Saxon fare in wood-panelled cellars serving a slice of history. Swim a little deeper into the city's gastro waters to fish out art nouveau brasseries, minimalist-style sushi bars and fusion cuisine.

In the centre, tuck into hearty local dishes in centuries-old taverns and vaulted cellars on Thomaskirchhof , Hainstrasse and the narrow streets fanning out from the market square. Barfussgässchen, Burgstrasse and Nikolaistrasse tempt with everything from shark steaks to filling *falafel*. With terraces on the cobblestones and pretty hidden courtyards, summer here spells alfresco dining with a Mediterranean feel.

Low-key and un-touristy, Gohlis comes first for affordable romance, fine dining and *Gose* beer, blending high-ceilinged art nouveau restaurants, intimate trattorias and snug gastro pubs. Waldstrasse boasts restaurants serving ethnic dishes such as spicy tacos and Thai curries, while Gohliser Strasse scores points for authentic French and local treats.

PRICE CATEGORIES

The restaurant price guides used in this book indicate the average cost of a three-course meal for one person, excluding drinks.

£ up to €20   ££ €20–35   £££ over €35

The south sizzles with a veritable cornucopia of quirky little restaurants, relaxed pubs and arty cafés with a boho vibe. Head for canalside Plagwitz to dine by the water's edge or in particularly charming converted red-brick factories. Südvorstadt's Karl-Liebknecht-Strasse and Münzgasse have a generous sprinkling of global flavours – from cheap-and-cheerful Chinese to Lebanese offerings.

Every Tuesday and Friday (09.00–17.00), local farmers set up shop on Markt (Market Square) and stalls overflow with tasty organic produce. This is the place to sniff out pungent cheeses, shiny fruit and vegetables, fresh fish and meat, crusty homemade breads, and pretty much whatever else takes your fancy.

For a true taste of Leipzig, munch on regional dishes that use simple but flavoursome ingredients. A favourite is *Leipziger Allerlei* (vegetable stew with crayfish tails and flour dumplings), washed back with citrusy Müller-Thurgau wines or tangy *Gose* beer. A meal is often rounded off with plenty of coffee, or *Scheelchen Heessen* as it's called locally.

Leipzig's array of pastries and pralines make mouths water and waistlines expand, so indulge now and diet tomorrow. The sweet-toothed should try *Leipziger Lerche* cakes, marzipan-and-plum stuffed *Leipziger Räbchen* dough balls rolled in cinnamon and *Quarkkeulchen* curd dumplings. Putting the culture into confectionery are *Bachpfeiffen*, coffee-coated pralines filled with cream and shaped like organ pipes, made in tribute to Bach.

Devotees of the checked blanket and the odd blade of grass in their sandwich will be delighted to learn that Leipzig has rich

LARKING AROUND

You're bound to see the *Leipziger Lerche* (Leipzig lark) on the menu at some point. This tasty speciality dates back to the 18th century when the dish was made with skylarks. Having developed a taste for songbirds, the locals would hunt migrating larks on the Elbe and Saale rivers in autumn, wrap them in bacon and serve them with *sauerkraut*. The practice was outlawed by the king of Saxony in 1876, following public protest, but a sweet version still exists. It is an entirely bird-free delight: a delicious cake made with shortcrust pastry, almonds, nuts and strawberry jam.

pickings in the picnic department. When the weather warms, fill your basket with local specialities and make for shady spots like Clara-Zetkin and Rosental parks. Lay your blanket on Lake Cospuden's beach or the Karl Heine Canal's banks. The Dübener Heide's wild heathlands and Auenwald woodlands offer a back-to-nature experience.

Many of Leipzig's restaurants, cafés and bars include a service charge in the bill, but it's normal to leave a small tip if you were pleased with the service. Locals usually round the bill off to the nearest euro or leave a tip of around five per cent for good or ten per cent for excellent service. In Germany, it's standard practice to tip waiters and waitresses when paying the bill, not by leaving the money on the table.

USEFUL DINING PHRASES

I would like a table for ... people, please
Ich möchte ein Tisch für ... Personen, bitte
Ikh merkhter ine teesh foor ... perzohnen, bitter

Waiter/waitress!	**May I have the bill, please?**
Herr Ober/Frau Kellnerin!	Die Rechnung, bitte?
Hair ohber/frow kell-nair-in!	*Dee rekhnung, bitter?*

I am a vegetarian. Does this contain meat?
Ich bin Vegetarier (Vegetarierin fem.). Enthält das hier Fleisch?
Ish bin veggetaareer (veggetaareerin). Enthelt dass heer flyshe?

Where is the toilet (restroom) please?
Wo sind die Toiletten, bitte?
Voo zeent dee toletten, bitter?

I would like a cup of/two cups of/another coffee/tea, please
Ich möchte eine Tasse/zwei Tassen/noch eine Tasse Kaffee/Tee, bitte
Ikh merkhter iner tasser/tsvy tassen/nok iner tasser kafey/tey, bitter

I would like a beer/two beers, please
Ich möchte ein Bier/Zwei Biere, bitte
Ikh merkhter ine beer/tsvy beerer, bitter

Entertainment & nightlife

When most cities start to snooze, Leipzig lets its hair down. Fuelled by late-night revellers and party-mad students, plenty of cheap drinks and late licensing in the wall-to-wall bars and clubs, this sleepless city has one of Germany's hippest and most active after-dark scenes.

The secret is its diversity – you can step from Bach cantatas in cobbled courtyards and cocktails on Barfussgässchen to salsa moves in Südvorstadt and mellow grooves in canal-crossed Plagwitz. Or how about an evening with a twist? Leipzig's passion for the weird and wonderful has seen kooky bars sprout up: you can sip *mojitos* lying on the floor at Sol y Mar (see page 74).

Bracing themselves for a big night, most locals begin the evening with a few drinks in the centre to gather momentum. The night kicks off around 23.00 when the bars lining Barfussgässchen fill up. If you want to hit the clubs, don't get there before midnight unless you want the dance floor to yourself.

Leipzig's cultural cup runs over and you will not be stuck for entertainment. it boasts theatres, concert halls, cinemas, cabaret clubs and avant-garde arts venues. From satirical comics to soprano singers, you're well catered for here.

To book tickets in advance, contact the venue direct or try **Ticket Shop** (ⓐ Arndtstrasse 10 ⓣ 0341 980 0098 ⓦ www.lvz-ticket.de), covering major festivals, gigs and performances.

The epicentre of the Drallewatsch pub mile – the narrow Barfussgässchen – feels Mediterranean, with music pumping out of every bar and alfresco drinking on the heated terraces. At weekends, the bars and basement clubs are loud and lively,

WHAT'S ON

The following websites feature more information about entertainment and nightlife in Leipzig:

Leipzig Tag & Nacht (Ⓦ www.leipzigtagundnacht.de) gives the lowdown on Leipzig's hippest bars, clubs and restaurants.

Z-Leipzig Online (Ⓦ www.z-leipzig-nachts.de) has the latest listings for Leipzig festivals, gigs, parties, theatre productions, film screenings and club nights.

so you'll often have to squeeze your way through the door. The theatre district around Gottschedstrasse scores points for its cult bars, quirky cafés and stand-up comedy, while Gohlis tempts those seeking *Gose* beer with its snug, wood-panelled taverns.

King of the alternative scene, Südvorstadt's Karl-Liebknecht-Strasse has a come-as-you-are feel that reels in the students. Expect everything from gothic cellars to psychedelic pubs in which DJs still spin vinyl. Nearby, the pub mile around Münzgasse and Peterssteinweg is chock-a-block with laid-back lounge bars that don't feel much bigger than a postage stamp. For a boho atmosphere, canal views and beer in converted red-brick factories, make for Plagwitz.

Clubbers who want to dance till dawn head for Barfussgässchen, where nightspots range from kitsch to ultra-cool. Names to look out for include basement jazz club Spizz (see page 76), and Saxony's so-called biggest ski chalet, Alpenmax (see page 75). Go south for infectious rhythms at Cuban Club Havana (see page 90).

Illuminated by night, Leipzig's two performing arts giants, the Gewandhaus (see page 66) and Opera House (see page 66) dominate either side of the sprawling Augustusplatz. This is also the site for plenty of open-air events like the free Classic Open festival in August, where classical, jazz and blues stars take to the stage and wow the crowds.

● *Barrels and bratwurst in the Auerbachs Keller*

Sport & relaxation

SPECTATOR SPORTS
Athletics
Leipzig Arena (ⓐ Am Sportforum ❶ Ticket hotline: 0341 234 1100 ⓦ www.arena-ticket.com) reveals the city's passion for athletics. Top-flight meetings and big-occasion events in all sports are held here.

Football
The jewel in the crown of football-mad Saxony, Leipzig has been having a ball ever since the then-VfB Leipzig won the cup at the first German championship in 1903. Just next door to the Arena and built to shine for the FIFA World Cup 2006, the state-of-the-art **Central Stadium** (ⓐ Am Sportforum ❶ Ticket hotline: 0341 234 1100 ⓦ www.sportforum-leipzig.com) can squeeze 45,000 spectators onto its terraces.

PARTICIPATION SPORTS
Swimming
When weather permits, take the plunge in Lake Kulkwitz's clean waters and open-air pools, or swim laps in Leipzig's Kleinzschocher and Gohlis lidos surrounded by greenery. No matter in which direction you head, you won't have to go far before you reach one of the city's many indoor pools.

Walking & cycling
Leipzig's plethora of parks and gardens, Lake Kulkwitz's promenade and the canal-crossed Auenwald floodplain forest

⬥ *All ages can enjoy outdoor pursuits*

are prime two-wheel and two-leg territory, spiralling out from
green spaces like the Clara-Zetkin-Park and Botanic Gardens,
walkers and cyclists can enjoy more than 200 km (124 miles)
of marked trails. Bike hire is available at the main station
(see page 51).

Watersports

Daredevils get their white-water thrills on dune-fringed
Lake Cospuden just south of Leipzig. Spanning 420 hectares
(1.6 sq miles), the lake has a watersports centre, where those
with the nerve, the inclination and the ability, can scuba-dive
beneath the water or kite-surf above it (**t** 0341 356 510
w www.leipzigseen.de). Even wetter and wilder is the nearby
Markkleeberg Kanupark (**a** Wildwasserkehre 1 **t** 0342 9714 1291
w www.kanupark-markkleeberg.com), where you can test out
not only your nerve but also your potential for a career in
hydrospeed rafting or freestyle canoeing.

RELAXATION
Spa

After all that strenuous exercise, even if you've only been
watching other people doing it, why not head for Markkleeberg's
lakefront saunas and solaria? For the ultimate unwind just ten
minutes' walk east of the centre, make for **Sachsen Therme**'s
warren of 100°C (212°F) saunas, steamy whirlpools and
treatment rooms (**a** Schongauer Strasse 19 **t** 0341 259 9920
w www.sachsentherme.de). You will emerge a stranger to
anxiety and ready to face the city's manifold attractions.

Accommodation

Whether your preference is for funky backpacker digs or grand
19th-century villas, Leipzig has accommodation to suit all tastes
and budgets. If your budget is limited, choose no-frills hostels in
the centre or family-run guesthouses with bags of character
just a short tram ride away. For those with a little cash to spare,
try contemporary hotels with original art or five-star spa hotels
for the ultimate unwind.

HOTELS

Am Ratsholz ££ Unwind in the sauna at this contemporary
hotel. Comfortable rooms all have cable TV, direct-dial phone,
safe and fully equipped kitchenette. ⓐ Anton-Zickmantel-
Strasse 44 (Plagwitz & Südvorstadt) ⓣ 0341 494 4500
ⓦ www.hotel-am-ratsholz.de ⓝ Tram: 3, 13

Galerie Hotel Leipziger Hof ££–£££ Discover the art of sleeping
at this tranquil hotel doubling up as a gallery with 200 original
works. Guests can unwind in the whirlpool, sauna and beer garden.
Take advantage of the wireless internet at just €5 per person for

PRICE CATEGORIES
The ratings below indicate the approximate cost of a room
for two people for one night.
£ up to €45   ££ €45–80   £££ over €80

the duration of your stay. ⓐ Hedwigstrasse 1–3 (The City Centre)
ⓣ 0341 69740 ⓦ www.leipziger-hof.de ⓝ Tram: 1, 3

Hotel Berlin ££–£££ Relax in the shady courtyard of this
hotel near the Vflkerschlachtdenkmal. The restaurant
serves a generous breakfast buffet. Guests enjoy free parking.
ⓐ Riebeckstrasse 30 (The City Centre) ⓣ 0341 267 3000
ⓦ www.hotel-berlin-leipzig.de ⓝ Tram: 4

Hotel Merseburger Hof ££–£££ This turreted, red-and-white
brick hotel oozes old-world grandeur. The plush rooms decked
out in greens and creams offer mod cons like wireless internet
access. Tuck into Saxon specialities in the restaurant and
enjoy the onsite bowling alley. ⓐ Merseburger Strasse 107
(The City Centre) ⓣ 0341 870 9660 ⓦ www.merseburger-hof.de
ⓝ Tram: 7

Mark Hotel Garni ££–£££ Put your feet up at this centrally located,
3-star hotel near the opera house. The bright apartments have
balconies. Ask the friendly, English-speaking staff for information
on Leipzig attractions and bike hire. ⓐ Gerichtsweg 12 (The City
Centre) ⓣ 0341 12780 ⓦ www.markhotelgarni.de ⓝ Tram: 4, 7

Vivaldi Hotel ££–£££ This Italian-style hotel is a home away from
home. Snug rooms with sleek drapes and chunky wood furniture
have cable TV and a minibar. Chill out in the courtyard restaurant.
ⓐ Wittenberger Strasse 87 (Gohlis & Zoo) ⓣ 0341 90360
ⓦ www.hotel-vivaldi.de ⓝ Tram: 16

Günnewig Hotel Vier Jahreszeiten £££ Expect a warm welcome at this cheery hotel near the station, where Leipzig's attractions are on your doorstep. Spacious, spotless rooms have comfy beds. Enjoy a hearty breakfast buffet in the light-filled conservatory. ⓐ Kurt-Schumacher-Strasse 23–29 (The City Centre) ⓣ 0341 98510 ⓦ www.guennewig.de ⓝ Train: Hauptbahnhof

Hotel Fürstenhof Leipzig £££ Blow the budget at Leipzig's most opulent hotel. This palatial building is all floor-to-ceiling glass and chandeliers. The icing on the 5-star cake

● Take in the sights from a city centre hotel

is the AquaMarin spa, with a landscaped pool and Roman steam bath. ⓐ Tröndlinring 8 (The City Centre) ⓣ 0341 1400 ⓦ www.luxurycollection.com/fuerstenhof ⓝ Tram: 1, 4, 12

Hotel Michaelis £££ Small but perfectly formed, this lovingly restored listed building is a find. Rooms have satellite TV and minibar. Not only that, but you can savour Mediterranean flavours in the terrace restaurant. ⓐ Paul-Gruner-Strasse 44 (The City Centre) ⓣ 0341 26780 ⓦ www.hotel-michaelis.de ⓝ Tram: 10, 11

Precise Accento Leipzig £££ This funky hotel provides a breath of fresh air with its Pop Art design and modern fitness centre with sauna. Expect rooms with bold colours and smooth contours. ⓐ Tauchaer Strasse 260 (The City Centre) ⓣ 0341 92620 ⓦ www.precisehotels.com ⓝ Tram: 9 (and then a 20 minute walk) or Tram: 9 (and then catch Bus: 82)

HOSTELS

Central Globetrotter £ Just minutes from Leipzig's central station, this no-curfew hostel has clean two- to eight-bed dorms. Facilities feature a communal kitchen, lockers, internet access and bar. ⓐ Kurt-Schumacher-Strasse 41 (The City Centre) ⓣ 0341 149 8960 ⓦ www.globetrotter-leipzig.de ⓝ Train: Hauptbahnhof

Hostel Sleep Lion £ The pick of the budget bunch, this laid-back hostel set in an attractive townhouse is in Leipzig's theatre district. Bike hire and internet access are available.

ⓐ Käthe-Kollwitz-Strasse 3 (The City Centre) ☎ 0341 993 9480
ⓦ www.hostel-leipzig.de Ⓝ Tram: 1, 14

GUESTHOUSES

Pension Ameta £ A good cheapie, this whitewashed townhouse is close to Clara-Zetkin Park. Light and airy, the self-catering rooms with wood floors and comfy beds have private bathrooms and kitchenettes. ⓐ Fichtestrasse 12 (Plagwitz & Südvorstadt) ☎ 0341 330 0000 ⓦ www.ameta-pension.de Ⓝ Tram: 10, 11

Abtnaundorfer Park ££ This family-run guesthouse located in an 18th-century villa and surrounded by leafy parkland has its own terrace, gardens and car park. Elegant rooms all have shower, phone, satellite TV and minibar. ⓐ Abtnaundorfer Strasse 61 ☎ 0341 232 7885 ⓦ www.apark.de Ⓝ Tram: 1

CAMPSITES

Camping Auensee £ Open year-round, this back-to-nature campsite has 168 pitches in the Auenwald woodlands. Enjoy outdoor activities like cycling and hiking. There is a sports field, children's playground and facilities for guests with special needs. ⓐ Gustav-Esche-Strasse 5 ☎ 0341 465 1600 ⓦ www.camping-auensee.de Ⓝ Bus: 80 (and then catch Tram 10 or 11)

Camping am Kulkwitzer See £ This peaceful spot overlooking Lake Kulkwitz's clear waters is about 6 km (4 miles) from the centre. Open from April to October, it has a bakery, playground, boat hire and lakeside restaurant. ⓐ Seestrasse 1 ☎ 0341 710 770 ⓦ www.kulkwitzer-see.de Ⓝ Tram: 1, 2, 15

THE BEST OF LEIPZIG

Whether you are on a flying visit to Leipzig, or taking a more leisurely break in Germany, the city offers some sights and experiences that should not be missed.

TOP 10 ATTRACTIONS

- **Auerbachs Keller** The whiff of sausages and hum of chatter hit you as you descend the staircase to this vast cellar, where Goethe found inspiration (see page 74)

- **Bach Museum** A symphony of Renaissance romance and Bach melodies, this museum strikes a chord with classical music lovers (see page 61)

- **Thomaskirche (St Thomas's Church)** Glimpse the cross-ribbed vaulting and Gothic nave at this 13th-century church, where Bach once conducted (see page 65)

- **Museum der Bildenden Künste (MDBK) (Museum of Fine Arts)** Max Klinger's marble *Beethoven* sculpture and works by Ruisdael and Rubens are amongst the treats at this light-flooded gallery (see page 66)

▼ *Cruising on the Karl Heine Canal*

- **Altes Rathaus (Town Hall)** Trace Leipzig's history behind the walls of this Renaissance edifice on Markt (see page 60)

- **Grassi Museum Complex** This cultural complex shelters a trio of museums, moving from musical instruments to applied art and ethnology (see page 67)

- **Rosental Park** Laze beside the fountains and hike over unspoilt heathland in this central pocket of greenery (see page 93)

- **Leipzig Opera House** Ballet dancers pirouette across the stage and world-class sopranos hit the high notes on Augustusplatz (see page 66)

- **Völkerschlachtdenkmal (Monument to the Battle of Nations)** Towering over Leipzig, this iconic stone giant commemorates the battle fought against Napoleon's forces (see page 83)

- **Gosenschenke Ohne Bedenken** Discover the delights of Leipzig's amber nectar with a glass of citrusy *Gose* in this wood-panelled cellar (see page 102)

Suggested itineraries

HALF-DAY: LEIPZIG IN A HURRY
Stroll past the Renaissance arches of the Altes Rathaus (Old Town Hall, see page 60) on the cobbled Markt (Market Square), pausing to gaze at the octagonal tower of Nikolaikirche (St Nicholas's Church, see page 64). Admire Dutch Masters in the MDBK (Museum of Fine Arts, see page 66), before enjoying beer and *Bratwurst* in the 16th-century wood-panelled Auerbachs Keller (see page 74).

1 DAY: TIME TO SEE A LITTLE MORE
A whirlwind musical tour takes in the Bach Museum (see page 61) and the 13th-century Thomaskirche (St Thomas's

⏶ *Art nouveau architecture is a feature of the city*

Church, see page 65), where Bach worked for 27 years as cantor.
After a dose of culture in the Grassi Museum's galleries (see
page 67), relax beside the Clara Zetkin Park's fountains with
a picnic (see page 79), then boutique shop in the elegant
Mädler Passage and Specks Hof arcades (see pages 69 and 70).
Round out your day on a classical high at the Gewandhaus,
the glass-walled concert hall (see page 66).

2–3 DAYS: TIME TO SEE MUCH MORE

You've devoured much of what the centre has to offer, so now
take a bite out of Leipzig's lesser-known corners. Head south for
sweeping panoramas at the Asisi Factory (see page 78) and to
see the lofty Monument to the Battle of Nations (see page 83):
climb 90 m (295 ft) to the top to enjoy far-reaching city views.
Take time out to hike or bike in the Auenwald forest or swim
in Lake Cospuden's clear waters.

Go west to Plagwitz (see page 87) to boat past red-brick
factories on the Karl Heine Canal and soak up the boho vibe
in this revamped industrial district. Stepping north, find peace
at Rosental Park (see page 93), elephants at the zoo and baroque
art at Gohlis Palace (see page 96).

LONGER: ENJOYING LEIPZIG TO THE FULL

If time is not an issue, linger for a while to savour Leipzig before
exploring the region's hidden gems. Northwest of Leipzig, Halle
(see page 106) is split in two by the snaking River Saale and
makes a great trip out.

Further north, castle-hop your way around the Dessau-Wörlitz
Gartenreich, a UNESCO World Heritage Site (see page 116).

Something for nothing

One of the reasons why Leipzig is flourishing as a city-break destination is its attractive value-for-money factor. Kick off your stay with an amble through the labyrinthine city centre, pausing to soak up the relaxed vibe beside the Renaissance Rathaus in the Markt (see page 60) and take a peek behind

● *Relive Leipzig's troubled past at the Stasi Museum*

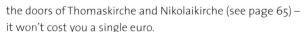

the doors of Thomaskirche and Nikolaikirche (see page 65) – it won't cost you a single euro.

Leipzig's high population of music students means the street performers here are practically pros. See them strum and serenade beside the Bach statue on Nikolaikirchhof, or take a stroll along Grimmaische Strasse to marvel at buskers, human statues, acrobats and jugglers. Pause for a budget snack from the mobile hotdog man near Galeria Kaufhof, who browns his sausages on a grill strapped to his front!

Trace Leipzig's fascinating history for free in the Stasi Museum (see page 67), home to the Stasi (secret police) headquarters until 1989. Meanwhile, culture vultures get occasional kicks from complimentary events at the Moritzbastei (see page 76), Leipzig's thrifty student honey-pot, staging everything from live jazz to improvised theatre (check the programme in advance). Drinks and snacks served here are among the cheapest in town.

It costs nothing to immerse yourself in art nouveau by wandering along Waldstrasse in Gohlis, which is lined with row upon row of beautifully restored townhouses. While you're in the mood for walking, go west to Rosental's Tower (see page 92), which peers above the treetops – the views over Leipzig from the top are worth the climb. Bring along something to eat to make the most of the park's shady picnic areas.

Summer in the city calls for lazy days on the beaches fringing Lake Kulkwitz, 20 minutes to the west of Leipzig, and long hikes in the cool Auenwald floodplain forest. A great alternative to the zoo is **Leipzig's wildlife reserve** (① 0341 309 410 ⓦ www.wildparkverein-leipzig.de), where you can observe European species in their near-to-natural habitat.

When it rains

With a host of indoor sights and shops, Leipzig never lets a sudden downpour dampen its spirits. Take shelter in one of the city's old-world coffee houses for a caffeine fix with a generous dollop of culture. The sublime Zum Arabischen Coffe Baum (see page 73) has pralines and pastries to take your mind off even the dreariest day. Nearby, Café Kandler (see page 71), overlooking Thomaskirche, brews creative teas named after great musicians – the ultimate wet-weather pick-me-up.

Shopping? Leipzig's got it covered. First up is the ultramodern Promenaden Hauptbahnhof mall (see page 70), where you can hop from one high-street store to the next. If designer labels are more up your street, make for the elegant Mädler Passage arcade (see page 69), where names like Aigner, Armani and Porsche Design tempt you to splash your cash.

Showers spell happy hours spent exploring Leipzig's top museums and galleries. For classical melodies, instruments and hands-on displays, the Bach Museum (see page 61) is a must. Allow enough time to take in the extensive collection at the Grassi Museum Complex (see page 67), spanning everything from hand-carved African artefacts to age-old harps. Those crazy about cars will love Rübesams Da Capo's shiny old-timers (see page 82), while bookworms can pore over the well-stocked shelves at the German National Library (see page 83).

Even when it's cold outside, one place pumping out plenty of warmth is Sachsen Therme spa (see page 36), where you can forget the drizzle by steaming and inhaling the essential oils (test out the oxygen and eucalyptus saunas), taking a dip in the effervescent whirlpools, or treating yourself to a soothing back scrub and rub.

If beer is more your thing than bubbles, snuggle up with a glass of *Gose* in Gosenschenke Ohne Bedenken's wood-panelled cellar (see page 102) or beside the Bayerischer Bahnhof's huge copper vats (see page 88). Ahhh, a few sips of the amber nectar and suddenly everything looks much brighter!

○ *The Grassi complex hosts a trio of interesting museums*

On arrival

TIME DIFFERENCE

Like the rest of Germany, Leipzig is on Central European Time (CET), an hour ahead of Greenwich Mean Time (GMT) in winter and British Summer Time (late Mar–end Oct).

ARRIVING

By air

Located 18 km (11 miles) from the centre, **Leipzig-Halle Airport** (ⓐ Leipzig-Halle Airport 1 ❶ 0341 224 1155 ⓦ www.leipzig-halle-airport.de) is the base for 25 airlines flying to 60 destinations across Germany and Europe, including Munich, London, Paris, Vienna and Madrid. Air Berlin offers budget deals, operating a daily service to London Stansted, Glasgow and Manchester.

Modern and user-friendly, the airport has an information desk, ATMs and car hire at Terminal B on the ground floor. There are also shops, restaurants, an internet access point, children's play area, florist and bakery.

The airport has good connections to central Leipzig. A speedy train service departs every 30 minutes from 03.50 to 23.50 for Leipzig and Halle, with the journey taking just 15 minutes. Taxis are readily available from the stand in front of Terminal B and should set you back around €18.

Lesser-known **Altenburg Airport** (ⓐ Am Flugplatz 1 ❶ 0344 7590 238 ⓦ www.flughafen-altenburg.de) is 45 km (28 miles) from Leipzig and served by no-frills airline Ryanair, flying daily to London Stansted. A shuttle bus links the airport to Leipzig and takes roughly 1 hour and 15 minutes.

By rail

It's a pleasure to pull into the immense **Leipzig Hauptbahnhof**
(ⓐ Willy-Brandt-Platz ⓦ www.bahnhof.de), the city's main station.
Deutsche Bahn ICE trains operate an hourly service to major
cities like Berlin (1 to 2 hours), Frankfurt (3 ½ to 4 hours), Munich
(4 ½ to 5 ½ hours) and Hamburg (3 to 3 ½ hours). There are also
direct connections to Dresden, Halle, Magdeburg, Dessau and
Wittenberg. If you're coming from Berlin, there's also a private
train line which offers cheap tickets from €12. The service runs
twice a day – in the early morning and late afternoon (for details,
see ⓦ www.interconnex.com).

Huge investment has created a state-of-the-art travel and
shopping experience at the station, which plays host to 140 shops,

🔺 *All aboard for a ride round Leipzig*

Around Leipzig

0   2km

0   1 mile

B2

B184

⑰

Leipzig
Messe

⑰

MOCKAU

TAUCHA

GOHLIS

Parthe

SCHÖNEFELD

⑱

⑲

B6

Leipzig Station
Hauptbahnhof

BORSDORF

LEIPZIG

ENGELSDORF

SÜDVORSTADT

MÖLKAU

THONBERG

A14

⑳

STÖTTERITZ

B86

Völkerschlachtdenkmal

HOLZHAUSEN

CONNEWITZ

PROBSTHEIDA

Parthe

N

MARKKLEEBERG

GROSSPÖSNA

Markkleeberger
See

✈ Leipzig-Altenburg

IF YOU GET LOST, TRY ...

Excuse me, do you speak English?
Entschuldigen Sie, sprechen Sie Englisch?
Entshuldigen zee, shprekhen zee english?

Excuse me, is this the right way to the old town/the city centre/the tourist office/the station/the bus station?
Entschuldigung, geht es hier zur Altstadt/zur Stadtmitte/zur Touristeninformation/zum Bahnhof/zum Busbahnhof?
Entshuldeegoong, gayt es here tsoor altshtat/tsoor shtatmitter/zur Touristeninformasion/tsoom baanhof/tsoom busbaanhof?

Can you point to it on my map, please?
Können Sie es mir bitte auf der Karte zeigen?
Kernen see es meer bitter owf der kaarte tsygen?

numerous cafés and restaurants and even a hair salon. If you need to store your luggage, there are lockers located below platform 3. There's an information desk to help with timetables and bookings.

By road
The bus station is in front of the Central Station. Eurolines and National Express serve a number of national and international destinations. Leipzig's public transport network, **Leipziger Verkehrsbetriebe** (ⓦ www.lvb.de), operates a long-distance bus service to German cities including Berlin.

Leipzig is well connected to Germany and the rest of Europe via the A9 (Berlin–Leipzig–Nuremberg–Munich) and A14 (Magdeburg–Leipzig–Dresden) motorways. The ring road that encircles Leipzig has 14 motorway junctions: follow the signs for Leipzig–Mitte to reach the centre.

Driving is hassle-free and parking affordable in Leipzig. The easiest option is to park in the main station's huge multi-storey car park, but make sure you have the right change as the ticket machine does not accept card payments.

FINDING YOUR FEET

Leipzig's residents are a friendly bunch, with a lively student population. The multicultural mix means that most locals speak good English and are happy to help travellers out. This is generally a safe city, but it's always wise to exert some caution, particularly in dimly lit areas at night.

ORIENTATION

Leipzig is easy to navigate. Coming out of the main train station, you'll find yourself in Mitte (the centre of town) where you can wander down cobblestone streets lined with old buildings. Catch a tram ten minutes south and you'll find yourself in Plagwitz and Südvorstadt. To the north in Gohlis and Zoo explore the lovely Rosental Park, catch some sport at Leipzig's famed Zentralstadion, or admire the expansive habitats for the animals at the Zoo.

GETTING AROUND

As most attractions cluster in the compact and largely pedestrianised centre, walking is often the quickest, easiest

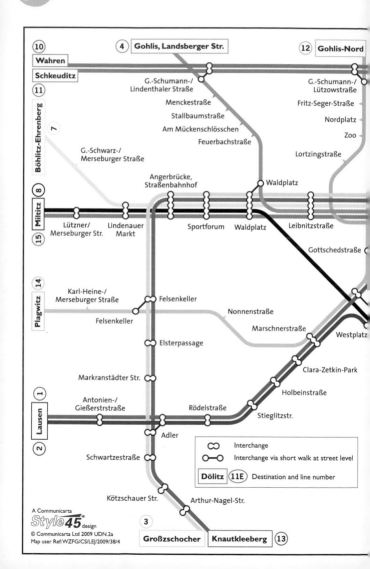

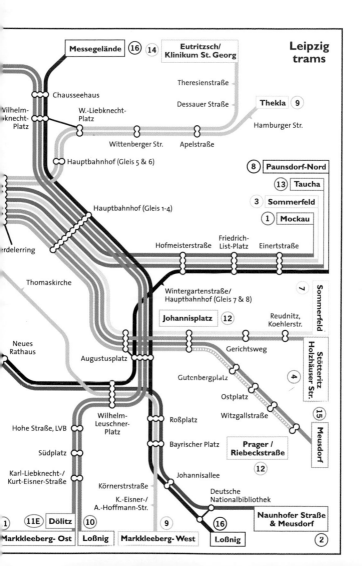

Leipzig trams

and cheapest way to explore. Pick up a free map from the tourist office.

Leipzig has 200 km (125 miles) of marked bike trails to explore. You can hire your own set of wheels from Fahrradladen Eckhardt (ⓐ Kurt-Schumacher-Strasse 4 ⓣ 0341 961 7274 ⓦ www.bikeandsport.info) behind the main station.

An extensive tram network criss-crosses the city. Make sure you validate your ticket at the stamping machine when boarding. If you're planning several trips, save with a day ticket for unlimited travel on public transport with Leipziger Verkehrsbetriebe (LVB).

Leipzig has 30 bus lines. It's worth investing in a one- to three-day Leipzig Welcome Card, which offers free travel on buses and trams, as well as discounts on the city's key attractions. It is available at a range of outlets including the Leipzig Information Centre, travel agents and many hotels, or online at ⓦ www.leipzig.de. Bus 89 is the city bus covering the centre's key attractions.

CAR HIRE

Avis ⓐ Ludwig-Erhard-Strasse 53 ⓣ 0341 259 580 ⓕ 0341 259 5825 ⓦ www.avis.com

Budget ⓐ Terminal 1 at Leipzig-Halle ⓣ 0341 224 1880 ⓕ 0341 224 1801 ⓦ www.budget.de

Europcar ⓐ Eutritzscher Strasse 24 ⓣ 0341 904 440 ⓕ 0341 904 4466 ⓦ www.europcar.com

Hertz ⓐ Terminal 1 at Leipzig-Halle ⓣ 0342 041 4317 ⓕ 0342 041 4390 ⓦ www.hertz.com

---

❍ *Augustusplatz displays Leipzig's modern edge*

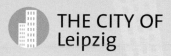

The City Centre

Mix jewel-box baroque buildings, cobbled inner courtyards and lofty Gothic churches with old-world arcades, pulsating nightlife and glass-fronted art galleries. Add a dash of Bach, a smidgen of Goethe, and there you have it: Leipzig city centre, a head-spinning cocktail of culture and contradictions.

SIGHTS & ATTRACTIONS

Ägyptisches Museum (Egyptology Museum)
Uncover mummies, funerary carvings and reliefs at this intriguing museum, part of the University of Leipzig. ⓐ Burgstrasse 21 ⓣ 0341 973 7010 ⓦ www.uni-leipzig.de ⓛ 13.00–17.00 Tues–Sat, 10.00–13.00 Sun & Mon ⓝ Tram: 4, 7, 9, 10, 11. Admission charge

Alte Handelsbörse (Old Stock Exchange)
This impressive building was built in the 17th century and was where merchant traders met for business. Today it's used mainly for concerts, lectures, festivals and private parties, so if you want to check out the inside, you'll need to get a ticket to one of these special events. ⓐ Naschmarkt ⓣ 0341 261 7766 ⓦ www.stadtgeschichtliches-museum-leipzig.de

Altes Rathaus (Old Town Hall)
The cream-and-terracotta Renaissance town hall dominating the market square is one of Germany's most beautiful, featuring a domed clock tower and arcades. Behind the sturdy walls, you'll find the Stadtgeschichtliches Museum. ⓐ Markt 1 ⓣ 0341 965 1320

Ⓦ www.stadtgeschichtliches-museum-leipzig.de ⏱ 10.00–18.00
Tues–Sun Ⓝ Bus: 89. Admission charge

Bach Museum
The Bosehaus is undergoing essential renovations (expected to
finish mid-2009), so there is a small interim Bach exhibition located
opposite in St. Thomas Church (Thomaskirche, see page 65).
ⓐ Thomaskirchhof 14 ⓣ 0341 913 7200 Ⓦ www.bach-leipzig.de
⏱ 11.00–18.00 Ⓝ Bus: 89; Tram: 9

🔺 *The attractive Altes Rathaus is home to the State History Museum*

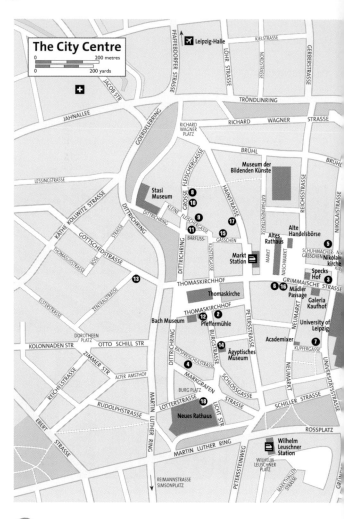

The City Centre

0   200 metres
0   200 yards

Leipzig-Halle

KIELSTRASSE

GERBESTRASSE

NORDSTRASSE

PFAFFEDORFER STRASSE

LÖHR STRASSE

TRÖNDLINRING

JACOB STR

JAHNALLEE

GOERDELERRING

RICHARD WAGNER PLATZ

RICHARD   WAGNER   STRASSE

BRÜHL

BRÜHL

LESSINGSTRASSE

Museum der Bildenden Künste

REICHSSTRASSE

NIKOLAISTRASSE

GROSSE FLEISCHERGASSE

HAINSTRASSE

KATHARINENSTRASSE

Stasi Museum

8

DITTRICHRING

KÄTHE KOLLWITZ STRASSE

10

KLEINE FLEISCHERGASSE

9

DITTRICHRING

11

DITTRICHRING

BARFUSS

15

GÄSSCHEN

17

Alte Handelsbörse

Altes Rathaus

SCHUHMACHER GÄSSCHEN

5

Nikolai-
kirche

3

GOTTSCHEDSTRASSE

ROSE STRASSE

ZENTRALSTRASSE

Markt Station

MARKT

MASCHMARKT

Specks Hof

THOMASSTRASSE

13

THOMASKIRCHHOF

GRIMMAISCHE STRASSE

6 **16**

Mädler Passage

NEUMARKT

Galeria Kaufhof

ELSTERSTRASSE

Thomaskirche

THOMASKIRCHHOF

2

University of Leipzig

DOROTHEEN PLATZ

Bach Museum

Pfeffermühle

PETERSSTRASSE

7

Academixer

KOLONNADEN STR

OTTO SCHILL STR

BURGSTRASSE

14

Ägyptisches Museum

KUPFERGASSE

NEUMARKT

ZIMMER STR

ALTER AMSTHOF

RATHERSCHULSTRASSE

DITTRICHRING

4

SCHLOSSGASSE

REICHELSTRASSE

MARKGRAFEN

BURG PLATZ

STRASSE

UNIVERSITÄTSSTRASSE

RUDOLPHSTRASSE

LOTTERSTRASSE

18

LICHT STR

SCHILLER STRASSE

Neues Rathaus

ROSSPLATZ

EBERT STRASSE

MARTIN LUTHER RING

MARTIN   LUTHER   RING

Wilhelm Leuschner Station

WILHELM LEUSCHNER PLATZ

REIMANNSTRASSE
SIMSONPLATZ

PETERSTEINWEG

GRÜNEWALDSTRASSE

MAXIMILIANSTRASSE

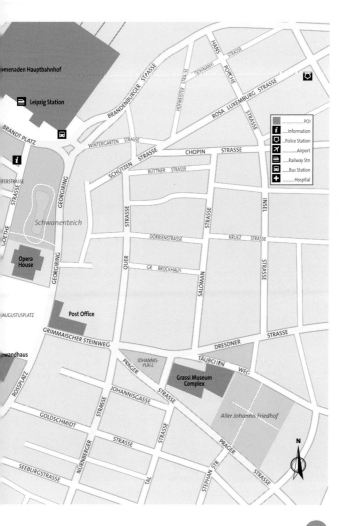

menaden Hauptbahnhof

Leipzig Station

BRANDT PLATZ

BRANDENBURGER STRASSE

HANS STRASSE

HOFMEISTER STRASSE

DOHNANYI STRASSE

PORCHE STRASSE

ROSA LUXEMBURG STRASSE

WINTERGARTEN STRASSE

SCHÜTZEN STRASSE

CHOPIN STRASSE

BÜTTNER STRASSE

TERSTRASSE

GEORGIRING

GOETHE STRASSE

Schwanenteich

STRASSE

STRASSE

INSEL

DÖRRIENSTRASSE

KRUEZ STRASSE

GEORGIRING

Opera House

QUER STRASSE

GR BROCKHAUS

SALOMAN STRASSE

STRASSE

AUGUSTUSPLATZ

Post Office

GRIMMAISCHER STEINWEG

DRESDNER STRASSE

ewandhaus

ROSSPLATZ

PRAGER STRASSE

JOHANNIS-PLATZ

TAURCHEN WEG

Grassi Museum Complex

JOHANNISGASSE

STRASSE

STRASSE

Aller Johannis Friedhof

GOLDSCHMIDT

NÜRNBERGER STRASSE

STRASSE

TAL STRASSE

PRAGER STRASSE

SEEBURGSTRASSE

STEPHAN STR

N

	POI
i	Information
	Police Station
✈	Airport
	Railway Stn
	Bus Station
✚	Hospital

Neues Rathaus (New Town Hall)

With its stone arches and silvery turrets, this vast neo-Renaissance town hall marks the spot where medieval Pleissenburg castle once stood. Climb up for sweeping views over Leipzig's rooftops. ⓐ Martin-Luther-Ring 4 ⓣ 0341 1230 ⓛ 10.00–18.00 Mon–Fri; guided tours at 11.00 & 14.00 ⓝ Tram: 9. Admission charge

⬤ *The home of the famous boys' choir: Thomaskirche*

Nikolaikirche (St Nicholas's Church)

Part Romanesque, part Gothic, this is where the 1989 Monday demonstrations took place that ultimately led to the reunification of Germany. ⓐ Nikolaikirchhof 3 ⓣ 0341 960 5270 ⓦ www.nikolaikirche-leipzig.de ⓛ 10.00–18.00 Mon–Sat; services: 09.30, 11.15, 17.00 Sun ⓝ Bus: 89

Thomaskirche (St Thomas's Church)

Bach worked as cantor for 27 years at this 13th-century church, where he now rests. Admire the cross-ribbed vaulting, Gothic nave, and marble-and-alabaster baptismal font. It's still home to the renowned St Thomas's Boys Choir. ⓐ Thomaskirchhof 18 ⓣ 0341 2222 4200 ⓦ www.thomaskirche.org ⓛ 09.00–18.00 ⓝ Bus: 89; Tram: 9

University of Leipzig

Founded in 1409, the University of Leipzig is one of the oldest universities in Europe. Among its famous pupils were Johann Wolfgang Goethe, Robert Schumann, Richard Wagner and Friedrich Nietzsche. Its various buildings are dotted around the city. ⓐ Universitätsstrasse/Augustusplatz/Ritterstrasse 26 ⓦ www.uni-leipzig.de ⓝ Tram: 7, 8, 10, 15

CULTURE

Academixer

If you speak some German, it is well worth catching a performance at this satirical cabaret and comedy venue. ⓐ Kupfergasse 2 ⓣ 0341 2178 7878 ⓦ www.academixer.com ⓛ Shop: 10.00–20.00; performances at 20.00 ⓝ Tram: 10, 11

Gewandhaus

The renowned Gewandhaus Orchestra takes the stage at this mighty glass-walled concert hall on Augustusplatz. In the foyer, see Europe's biggest ceiling fresco, Sighard Gille's *Song of Life*.
ⓐ Augustusplatz 8 ❶ 0341 12700 ⓦ www.gewandhaus.de ⓛ Box office: 10.00–18.00 Mon–Fri, 10.00–14.00 Sat ⓝ Tram: 7, 10, 12, 15

Museum der Bildenden Künste – MDBK (Museum of Fine Arts)

This crystalline cube reflects Michael Fischer-Art's work covering the buildings opposite. Seek out Max Klinger's striking *Beethoven* sculpture (1885), shaped from marble, alabaster and bronze. Other highlights include works by Dutch Masters and Impressionists, plus Ecker's oversized red whistles.
ⓐ Katharinenstrasse 10 ❶ 0341 216 990 ⓦ www.mdbk.de
ⓛ 10.00–18.00 Tues & Thur–Sun, 12.00–20.00 Wed ⓝ Train: Hauptbahnhof. Admission charge

Opera House

Illuminated by night, Leipzig's opera house on Augustusplatz opened in 1960 on the site of the New Theatre which suffered extensive bomb damage during World War II. The repertoire ranges from opera and musicals to cutting-edge ballet.
ⓐ Augustusplatz 12 ❶ 0341 126 1261 ⓦ www.oper-leipzig.de
ⓛ Box office: 08.00–20.00 Mon–Fri, 10.00–16.00 Sat
ⓝ Tram: 4, 7, 8, 10, 11, 12, 15, 16

Pfeffermühle

Satirical cabaret in the courtyard is the appeal of this atmospheric bar and comedy club, housed in the baroque Bosehaus.

GRASSI MUSEUM COMPLEX

There are three museums within the Grassi complex:
The Museum of Applied Arts, The Museum of Ethnology
and the Museum of Musical Instruments. The exhibits
range from textiles, ceramics and furniture to African
artefacts and Renaissance lutes. Highlight: after seeing
all the antique instruments behind glass, you can go
upstairs and play some. Great for the kids, but fun for
adults, too. ⓐ Johannisplatz 5–11 ❶ 0341 222 9100
ⓦ www.grassimuseum.de ❶ 10.00–18.00 Tues–Sun
ⓝ Tram: 4, 7, 12, 15. Admission charge

ⓐ Thomaskirchhof 16 ❶ 0341 960 3196 ⓦ www.kabarett-
leipziger-pfeffermuehle.de ❶ 18.00 until end of show ⓝ Tram: 9

Stasi Museum

Home to Leipzig's Stasi (secret police) headquarters until
1989, this round-cornered building offers a fascinating
(albeit rather sinister) insight into Germany's troubled past.
Particularly creepy are the Stasi listening devices, the system
of letter interception and the scent jars (for dog-tracking).
While entry is free, donations are welcome. Guided tours
in English are possible for around €3 per person, but must
be booked in advance. ⓐ Dittrichring 24 ❶ 0341 961 2443
ⓦ www.runde-ecke-leipzig.de ❶ 10.00–18.00 ⓝ Tram: 3, 7, 15

RETAIL THERAPY

Bodo Zeidler im Alten Rathaus This dinky boutique is one of
the best places to shop for blue-and-white Meissener porcelain.
ⓐ Markt 1 ⓣ 0341 960 1714 ⓦ www.bodo-zeidler.de ⓛ 10.00–19.00
Mon–Fri, 10.00–16.00 Sat ⓝ Bus: 89

🔺 *Glass and glamour in the Promenaden Hauptbahnhof*

Galeria Kaufhof Find everything under one roof at this department store giant. ⓐ Neumarkt 1 ⓣ 0341 22450 ⓦ www.galeria-kaufhof.de ⓛ 09.30–20.00 Mon–Sat ⓝ Tram: 7, 10

Heidrich & Zeidler Seiffener Volkskunsterzeugniss There's a year-round smell and feel of Christmas at this Lilliputian shop selling handmade matchbox toys, wooden pyramids and traditional Erzgebirge decorations. ⓐ Markt 1 ⓣ 0341 124 8347 ⓛ 10.00–19.00 Mon–Fri, 10.00–16.00 Sat ⓝ Bus: 89

La Barrica Spanish specialities from Manchego cheese to Rioja wines share shelf space at this hole-in-the-wall gourmet shop opposite St Nicholas's Church. It's a good place to stock up on tapas for a picnic. ⓐ Ritterstrasse 4 ⓣ 0341 961 4334 ⓛ 12.00–20.00 Mon–Fri, 12.00–18.00 Sat ⓝ Bus: 89

Mädler Passage Whether you're seeking twinkling Swarovski, Marc O'Polo, Lacoste or Mandarina Duck, the sleek boutiques lining Leipzig's most elegant arcade come up with the goods. This is also a pleasant spot to rest your feet and enjoy a light lunch or coffee. ⓐ Mädler Passage, Grimmaische Strasse 2–4 ⓣ 0341 216 340 ⓦ www.maedler-passage-leipzig.de ⓛ 10.00–19.00 Mon–Fri, 10.00–18.00 Sat ⓝ Bus: 89

Meinosten This shop offers a range of kitsch East-German products from toys, t-shirts, postcards and sweets to souvenirs featuring the much-loved *Ampelmann* character. If you're looking for a present, check out the *Ostpakets* (gift boxes of

sweets). ⓐ Nikolaistrasse 42/Laden 8 ⓣ 0341 3373 4568
ⓦ www.meinosten.de ⓛ 10.00–20.00 Mon–Sat ⓝ Bus: 89;
Train: Hauptbahnhof

Petersbogen Opposite the New Town Hall, this modern glass
mall houses a cinema and casino, plus a string of clothing
and shoe shops. Visitors who are all shopped out thus have
many relaxation options. ⓐ Petersstrasse 36–44 ⓣ 0341 217 1785
ⓦ www.petersbogen.com ⓛ 10.00–20.00 Mon–Sat ⓝ Tram: 2,
8, 9, 10, 11

Promenaden Hauptbahnhof The main station's gleaming mall
shelters over 80 shops that stay open late, stocking everything
from fashion to fresh flowers and fine wines. ⓐ Willy-Brandt-
Platz 7 ⓣ 0341 141 270 ⓦ www.promenaden-hauptbahnhof-
leipzig.de ⓛ 09.30–22.00 Mon–Sat, 13.00–18.00 Sun ⓝ Train:
Hauptbahnhof

Schmuckwerk Hübener If you're looking for jewellery with an
edge, then you've found the right place. The collection includes
unique rings, bangles, earrings and necklaces from contemporary
German designers. ⓐ Altes Rathaus, Naschmarkt ⓣ 0341 961 5278
ⓦ www.schmuckwerk-huebener.de ⓛ 11.00–20.00 Mon–Fri,
11.00–19.00 Sat ⓝ Bus: 89; Train: Hauptbahnhof

Specks Hof Murals, courtyards and narrow passages define
Leipzig's oldest arcade, the place to come for designer wear
and original art. ⓐ Reichsstrasse 4–6 ⓣ 0341 149 1761
ⓛ 08.00–20.00 Mon–Fri, 08.00–18.00 Sat ⓝ Tram: 7, 10

TAKING A BREAK

Bagel Brothers £ ❶ If you're looking for healthier fast food, this bagel chain serves up a variety of fresh bagels, chicken fajitas, homemade cakes and frozen yoghurts. ⓐ Nikolaistrasse 42 ❶ 0341 980 3330 ⓦ www.bagelbrothers.com ⓒ 06.30–23.30 Mon–Thur, 06.30–02.00 Fri, 07.30–02.00 Sat, 08.30–23.30 Sun ⓝ Train: Hauptbahnhof

Café Kandler £ ❷ Choose from an assortment of over 80 different teas, including the special Bach tea. And if you have a sweet tooth, you can't go past the *Leipziger Lerche* cakes or *Bachtaler* pralines. ⓐ Thomaskirchhof 11 ❶ 0341 213 2181 ⓒ 06.30–02.00 ⓝ Tram: 9

Eiscafe San Remo £ ❸ From the classics like chocolate, vanilla and strawberry, to passionfruit and yoghurt, mango and melon, this *gelato* bar offers 48 different homemade flavours. They also serve special ice cream cups, *frappes* and milkshakes. For a cool summer cocktail try a *Sektbecher Orange*, with lemon sorbet and orange juice. ⓐ Nikolaistrasse 1 ❶ 0341 211 1772 ⓒ 10.00–22.00 Mon–Sat, 10.00–21.00 Sun ⓝ Tram: 9

Grotta la Pallazzese £ ❹ Savour Italian specialities at this establishment that's decorated with stalagmites. Be sure to taste their unique gelato flavours that range from poppy and marzipan to basil. ⓐ Ratsfreischulstrasse 6–8 ❶ 0341 962 9974 ⓦ www.lagrottaleipzig.de ⓒ 11.00–00.00 ⓝ Tram: 9

Kaffeehaus Riquet £ ❺ Elephant heads guard the door at this Viennese-style café, with its dark polished wood and sweeping staircase. ⓐ Schuhmachergässchen 1 ❶ 0341 961 0000 ⓦ www.riquethaus.de ⓛ 09.00–22.00 ⓝ Bus: 89

Kümmel Apotheke £ ❻ This stylish café-bar-bistro with polished floorboards serves up hearty meals and a range of coffee and cocktails. ⓐ Mädler Passage ❶ 0341 960 8705 ⓦ www.kuemmel-apotheke.de ⓛ 10.00–00.00 ⓝ Tram: 9

Mokkaflip £ ❼ Located opposite the university, this comfy student hangout offers free Wi-Fi and all-day breakfasts, as well as a selection of milkshakes, smoothies and iced coffee.

DRALLEWATSCH

Saxon slang for pub-crawl, the *Drallewatsch* centres around the bustling Barfussgässchen and Fleischergasse, where wall-to-wall bars, clubs, restaurants and open-air cafés vie for your attention. Things heat up about midnight when Leipzig's party people brace themselves for a big night out with cocktails on the terrace – try Bellini's or the Duke Bar – before moving onto a live concert in Spizz or Bar Fusz. Next up are clubs like Madrigal where revellers dance to everything from Russian disco to R'n'B grooves. The good news for night-owls is that most places on the bar mile have 24-hour licensing, referred to locally as 'open end', which means that the fun only stops when your feet do!

a Universitätsstrasse 16 **t** 0341 999 5555 **w** www.mokkaflip.de
l 10.00–20.00 Mon–Sat, 11.00–18.00 Sun **n** Tram:7, 10, 13, 15

El Espanol £–££ ❽ Located in the city centre, this restaurant will
sort you out with Spanish classics, from tapas to paella. **a** Grosse
Fleischergasse 19 **t** 0341 268 9427 **l** 18.00–late **n** Tram: 1, 7, 15

Zum Arabischen Coffe Baum ££ ❾ One of Europe's oldest coffee
houses encompasses three cafés, three restaurants and a fine
Café Museum. **a** Kleine Fleischergasse 4 **t** 0341 961 0060
w www.coffebaum.de **l** Pub & restaurant: 11.00–00.00;
Cafés & Café Museum: 11.00–19.00 **n** Tram: 9

AFTER DARK

RESTAURANTS
Mr Moto £ ❿ Leipzig's first *kaiten* sushi bar – often known
as conveyor-belt sushi. Here you sit around a bar, in front of a
little moat, choosing from plates of delicious morsels drifting
past on tiny boats. **a** Grosse Fleischergasse 21 **t** 0341 212 7898
w www.moto-sushi.de **l** 11.00–00.00 Mon–Sat, 11.00 23.00 Sun
n Tram: 12

Osteria Don Camillo & Peppone £ ⓫ This well-loved Italian
restaurant is cosy and not too pricey. Feast on a wide selection
of antipasti (duck liver, champignons and rocket), traditional
pasta dishes (*arrabiata*), great pizza and delicious tiramisu.
a Barfussgässchen 11 **t** 0341 960 3910 **w** www.doncamillo-
leipzig.de **l** 11.00–23.30 Mon–Sat, 17.00–23.30 Sun **n** Bus: 89

Restaurant Centralapotheke £ ⓬ Here you can eat *Leipziger Allerlei* stew and drink *Gose* beer on a terrace facing St Thomas's Church. There is also an Apotheke Museum for fans of the pharmacy. ⓐ Thomaskirchhof 12 ⓣ 0341 211 8299 ⓦ www.restaurant-centralapotheke.de ⓛ 11.00–00.00 ⓝ Tram: 9

Sol y Mar £ ⓭ Eat lying down in this ultra-sleek restaurant. Cream drapes, plush cushions and Balinese furniture create a relaxed mood, and you can even have a massage before dinner. ⓐ Gottschedstrasse 4 ⓣ 0341 961 5721 ⓦ www.solymar-leipzig.de ⓛ 09.00–late ⓝ Tram: 14

Thüringer Hof £ ⓮ Martin Luther and Schumann once frequented this 500-year-old restaurant, where you can dine on *Eisbein* (pickled pork with *sauerkraut*) beneath a vaulted ceiling. ⓐ Burgstrasse 19 ⓣ 0341 994 4999 ⓦ www.thueringer-hof.de ⓛ 11.00–00.00 ⓝ Tram: 9

Varadero £ ⓯ Shark steaks and garlicky gambas land on your plate in this funky Cuban restaurant. ⓐ Barfussgässchen 8 ⓣ 0341 960 0926 ⓛ 11.00–00.00 ⓝ Tram: 9

Auerbachs Keller ££ ⓰ This cavernous 16th-century cellar, Leipzig's most famous restaurant, was a favourite haunt of Goethe, who penned *Faust* here. Tuck into *Tafelspitz* (braised beef) with potato dumplings. ⓐ Mädler Passage ⓣ 0341 216 100 ⓦ www.auerbachs-keller-leipzig.de ⓛ 11.30–00.00 ⓝ Bus: 89

Barthels Hof ££ ⓱ Sample spit-roasted pork and salted herrings in this 500-year-old restaurant's inner courtyard. ⓐ Hainstrasse 1 ⓣ 0341 141 310 ⓦ www.barthels-hof.de ⓛ 07.00–00.00 ⓝ Bus: 89

Ratskeller ££ ⓲ Vaulted ceilings and stone arches set the scene in this art nouveau restaurant. ⓐ Lotterstrasse 1 ⓣ 0341 123 4567 ⓦ www.ratskeller-leipzig.de ⓛ 11.00–23.00 Mon–Sat, 11.00–15.30 Sun ⓝ Bus: 89; Tram: 2, 8, 9, 10, 11

BARS & CLUBS

Alpenmax Full of scantily-clad staff (the few suggestions of clothing that they wear hint at a mountain theme), this raucous club is dubbed Saxony's biggest ski chalet. A good place to meet a lonely goatherd of either gender, but not ideal for striking up a meaningful dialogue. ⓐ Grosse Fleischergasse 12 ⓣ 0341 224 8605 ⓛ 22.00–05.00 Mon–Sat ⓝ Tram: 12

Bar Fusz Bursting at the seams at weekends, this bar is hot, loud and happening. Party-goers spill out onto the heated terrace. Catch live bands here every second Wednesday night. ⓐ Barfussgässchen 6 ⓣ 0341 962 8624 ⓛ 09.00–02.00 Mon–Fri, 09.00–late Sat & Sun ⓝ Bus: 89

Bellini's Smooth funk plays as you sip a blackberry margarita in this lively cocktail bar, decked out with black-and-white pictures of jazz legends. ⓐ Barfussgässchen 3–5 ⓣ 0341 961 7681 ⓦ www.bellinis-leipzig.de ⓛ 12.00–late ⓝ Bus: 89

Kildare City Pub If you've got a craving for Guinness, fish 'n' chips (on a Tuesday) and big-screen sports, this cheery Irish pub hits the spot. Barfussgässchen 3–7 0341 983 9740 www.kildare.de 12.00–late Bus: 89

Madrigal This bar is a good option to relax and re-energise before moving on to more bars or a club. There's a range of wine, beer, juice (a selection of 15 different kinds for those abstaining from the falling-down lotion) and a decent cocktail list. Happy Hour is from 18.00–20.00. Käthe-Kollwitz-Strasse 10 0341 224 8546 18.00–late Mon–Sat Tram: 1

Mephisto At this addition to the Auerbachs Keller you can sway to live jazz and sip cocktails at the Goethe-inspired bar. Look into the mirror to hear the devilish Mephisto cackle. Mädler Passage, Grimmaische Strasse 2 0341 216 1022 www.auerbachs-keller-leipzig.de 11.00–late Bus: 89

Moritzbastei Located in the only remaining part of the old city walls, this student-run rabbit-warren of venues opens out into a central courtyard. It's an integral part of Leipzig's music and culture scene. On any given night you might find theatre, dance or an exhibition. Take part in a discussion or dance to local and international DJs and live acts. Universitätsstrasse 9 0341 702 590 www.moritzbastei.de 10.00–late Mon–Fri, 12.00–late Sat, 09.00–late Sun Tram: 7, 10, 13, 15

Spizz Jazz & Music Club Sip a mango *daiquiri* on the terrace, and then head for the basement to catch live blues and jazz acts, or DJs mixing up funk, soul and disco. ⓐ Markt 9 ⓣ 0341 960 8043 ⓦ www.spizz.org ⓛ 09.00–late ⓝ Bus: 89

Zur Pleissenburg Blink and you'll miss this quirky low-ceilinged watering hole full of local flavour. So don't blink. ⓐ Ratsfreischulstrasse 2 ⓣ 0341 960 2653 ⓛ 09.00–05.00 ⓝ Tram: 9

⬤ Have a devilish time at Mephisto

Plagwitz & Südvorstadt

A stark contrast to the north's art nouveau and the centre's baroque grandeur, Leipzig's sassy south has an urban edge and a boho vibe. The cogs and wheels of this once industrial area have been turned towards modern art and cutting-edge culture, transforming red-brick factories into galleries, chichi restaurants and buzzy bars.

SIGHTS & ATTRACTIONS

Asisi Factory Panometer

Architect and artist Yadegar Asisi's great love is creating huge (as in the largest on the planet) 360° panorama paintings depicting subjects from Mount Everest to Ancient Rome. The paintings are accompanied by informative exhibitions. ⓐ Richard-Lehmann-Strasse 114 ⓣ 0341 121 3396 ⓦ www.asisi-factory.de ⓛ 09.00–19.00 Tues–Fri, 10.00–20.00 Sat & Sun ⓝ Bus: 70; Tram: 9, 16

Botanischer Garten (Botanic Gardens)

Neat and petite, the University of Leipzig's botanic gardens are Germany's oldest, dating back to 1542. Wander the themed gardens to spot species like European orchids and the South American *Gunnera chilensis*, resembling a giant rhubarb. The greenhouses nurture cacti, ferns and many different butterfly varieties. ⓐ Linnestrasse 1 ⓣ 0341 973 6850 ⓦ www.unileipzig.de/bota ⓛ 09.00–16.00 Nov–Feb; 09.00–18.00 Mar & Apr, Oct; 09.00–20.00 May–Sept; hothouse: 13.00–16.00

Tues–Fri, 10.00–16.00 Sat, Sun & public holidays, Oct–Apr;
13.00–18.00 Tues–Fri, 10.00–18.00 Sat, Sun & public holidays,
May–Sept ⓝ Tram: 2, 16. Admission charge for the hothouse

Bundesverwaltungsgericht (Federal Administrative Court)

While a court may not top your sightseeing list, it's worth
making an effort to see this one. This grand neo-Renaissance
edifice overshadows Simsonplatz, with its soaring columns,
domes and sculpted lions. Take a peek inside to glimpse
the frescoed ballroom. ⓐ Simsonplatz 1 ⓣ 0341 20070
ⓦ www.bverwg.de ⓛ 16.00–18.00 Mon–Fri, 09.00–17.00 Sat
& Sun ⓝ Tram: 9, 10, 11 ⓘ To see inside you must register online.
To do this you'll need to know some German, or get help from
a German speaker

Clara-Zetkin Park

Sliced in two by the White Elster River, this expansive park to
the southwest of the centre is an oasis of calm. Thick canopies
of plane and beech trees provide welcome shade on hot days.
Relax beside the fountains and roses in the pretty Palmengarten.
ⓐ Karl-Tauchnitz-Strasse ⓣ 0341 123 6099 ⓝ Tram: 1, 2

Museum für Druckkunst (Museum of Printing Art)

Trace Leipzig's centuries-old printing history at this hands-on
museum in Plagwitz, housed in a red-brick factory. Interactive
displays give an insight into publishing industry techniques.
ⓐ Nonnenstrasse 38 ⓣ 0341 231 620 ⓦ www.druckkunst-
museum.de ⓛ 10.00–17.00 Mon–Fri, 11.00–17.00 Sun ⓝ Tram:
1, 2, 3, 14. Admission charge

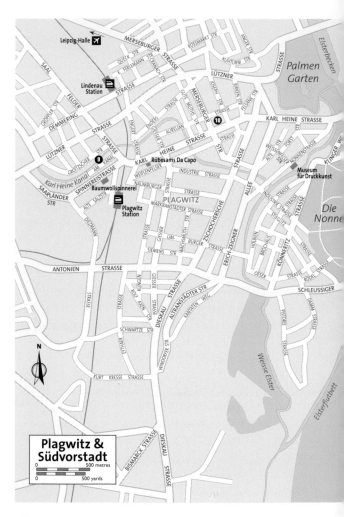

Leipzig-Halle

MERSEBURGER STRASSE

ROSSMARKT STR

ANGER STR

QUICK STR

KUHTURM STR

STRASSE

Palmen
Garten

Elsterbecken

SAAL

FELDER

COOPLER STR

DEMMERING

STRASSE

Lindenau
Station

K. FERLEMANN STR

E. SCHUNCK STR

STRASSE

LÜTZNER

MERSEBURGER

BIRKEN STR

FELSANE STR

JOSEPH STR

STRASSE

STRASSE

KARL HEINE STRASSE

LÜTZNER

STRASSE

ENGERT STRASSE

GROTZSCHER STR

GUTS MUTHS STR

GROSSE STR

AURELIAN

KARL HEINE STRASSE

STR

10

ALTE SALZ STR

WEISSENFEL

VOIGT STR

NONNENSTRASSE

KLINGER WEG

Kari Heine Kanal

AM KANAL

9

Rübesams Da Capo

WEFLENFELDER

INDUSTRIE STRASSE

Museum
für Druckkunst

SPINNEREISTRASSE

Baumwollspinnerei

NAUMBURGER

STRASSE

STRASSE

PLAGWITZ

ALLEE

INDUSTRIE STRASSE

STILGITZ

Die
Nonne

SAARLÄNDER
STR

Plagwitz
Station

MARKRANSTÄDTER STRASSE

STR

DICHAUN

MARKRANSTÄDTER STRASSE

GIESSER STR

WACHSMUTH

LIM-
BURGER STR

ZSCHOCHERSCHE

STIGLITZ

HOLBEIN

KÖNNERITZ

BROCKHAUS

RÖDEL STR

Elsterflutbett

ANTONIEN STRASSE

STR

SIEMENS STR

STR

ERICH-ZEIGNER

OESER

STRASSE

SCHLEUSSIGER

TASSELSTR

GIESSER STRASSE

KLINGER STRASSE

ROLE AXEN STR

DIESKAU STRASSE

ALTRANSTÄDTER STR

KANTATON WEG

DAMM STRASSE

PISTORIS STR

STRASSE

SCHWARTZE STR

ELTHAER STR

WINDORFER STR

DIESKAU

Weisse Elster

N

KURT KRESSE STRASSE

BISMARCK STRASSE

DIESKAU

STRASSE

Plagwitz &
Südvorstadt

0   500 metres

0   500 yards

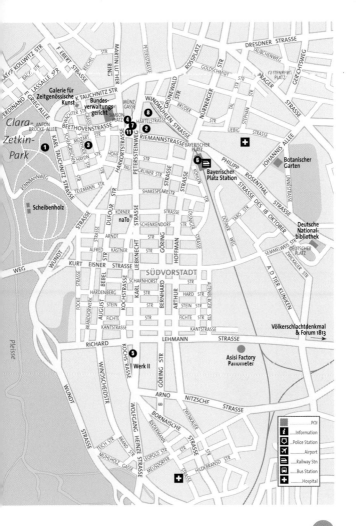

Rübesams Da Capo

Check out this vintage car museum (look out for the Interflug plane on the roof), where old-timers gleam against the backdrop of a beautifully restored red-brick factory. ⓐ Karl-Heine-Strasse 105 ⓣ 0341 926 0137 ⓦ www.ruebesams-dacapo.de ⓒ 11.00–18.00 Wed–Sat, 10.00–18.00 Sun ⓝ Bus: 72, 73; Tram: 14. Admission charge

Scheibenholz

Place a bet at this 140-year-old horse-racing track, Leipzig's oldest sports venue. Bordering Clara-Zetkin-Park, this venue is open during the racing season (May to October). ⓐ Rennbahnweg 2

● *Get in a spin at this old cotton mill, Baumwollspinnerei*

🕐 0341 960 4327 🌐 www.galoppimscheibenholz.de 🕐 12.00–19.00
🚊 Tram: 10,11 ❗ Check the website for racing day details

Volkerschlachtdenkmal (Monument to the Battle of Nations)

Soaring above Leipzig, this grey monolith was built to
commemorate the 100th anniversary of the Battle of the
Nations against Napoleon's troops. Guarded by a statue of
St Michael, the 96 m (315 ft) high memorial's viewing platform
affords far-reaching views over Leipzig. Both the huge stone
sculptures and the climb to the top are breathtaking. Audio
guides are available in German, English and French. 🅰 Prager
Strasse 🕐 0341 241 6870 🌐 www.voelkerschlachtdenkmal.de
🕐 10.00–18.00 Apr–Oct; 10.00–16.00 Nov–Mar 🚊 Tram: 2, 15.
Admission charge

CULTURE

Baumwollspinnerei

Housed in a former cotton mill, this labyrinthine venue comprises
a string of cavernous halls staging events from improvised
theatre to jazz concerts. The galleries showcase works by local
and international artists. 🅰 Spinnereistrasse 7 🕐 0341 498 0270
🌐 www.spinnerei.de 🕐 12.00–18.00 Tues–Fri, 11.00–18.00 Sat
🚊 Tram: 14

Deutsche National-bibliothek (German National Library)

Dominating Deutscher Platz, this huge building is festooned
with portraits of Goethe and Gutenberg (Johannes, not Steve).
For 120 years, the museum has collected, preserved and indexed

books and scripts, and is the oldest museum of its kind in the
world. ⓐ Deutscher Platz 1 ⓣ 0341 22710 ⓦ www.d-nb.de
ⓛ 09.00–16.00 Mon–Sat ⓝ Tram: 2, 16

Forum 1813

Next to the Monument to the Battle of the Nations, this
museum recounts the historic events leading up to the battle
in 1813. You'll need an extra ticket to see the 350 objects on
display, which include a model of Leipzig on a scale of 1:72.
Some explanations are given in English. ⓐ Prager Strasse
ⓣ 0341 241 6870 ⓦ www.stadtgeschichtliches-museum-
leipzig.de ⓛ 10.00–18.00 Apr–Oct; 10.00–16.00 Nov–Mar
ⓝ Tram: 2, 15. Admission charge

Galerie für Zeitgenössische Kunst (Contemporary Art Gallery)

Avant-garde art graces the stark white walls at this multimedia
gallery, sheltering contemporary paintings, photography and
sculpture. Most of the permanent collection dates back to Leipzig's
GDR times. ⓐ Karl-Tauchnitz-Strasse 9–11 ⓣ 0341 140 8126
ⓦ www.gfzk.de ⓛ 12.00–19.00 Tues–Sun ⓝ Tram: 2, 8. Admission
charge

naTo

Film, theatre, literature, politics and music push the boundaries
of convention at this arts centre. The offerings range from
experimental jazz to Tibetan overtone singing, but the venue
also stages fun summer events like the bathtub race and
soapbox derby. ⓐ Karl-Liebknecht-Strasse 46 ⓣ 0341 301 4397
ⓦ www.nato-leipzig.de ⓝ Tram: 10, 11

Werk II

Catch alternative events like the Leipzig Pop-Up Festival
(see page 12), as well as theatre and live music from local
acts to international oufits like the Stereophonics and Bad
Religion in this 19th-century brick building. ⓐ Kochstrasse 132
ⓣ 0341 308 0140 ⓦ www.werk-2.de ⓛ Check website for
individual event details ⓝ Tram: 9, 10, 11

RETAIL THERAPY

Graue Maus Local designer Maria Schenke's creations
are both beautiful and functional. They are also creative –
her designs combine futuristic materials with classic lines.
ⓐ Karl-Liebknecht-Strasse 50 ⓣ 0341 983 2170 ⓦ www.graue-
maus.de ⓛ 12.00–19.00 Mon–Thur, 12.00–16.00 Fri ⓝ Tram: 11

Miufeij Miufeij creates all her pieces by hand using merino
wool and silk in the traditional art of felt-making. She creates
skirts, dresses and tops, as well as bags, scarves, caps and
jewellery. ⓐ Spinnereistrasse 7, Hall 18, Room 3 ⓣ 0177 614 1246
ⓦ www.miufeij.de ⓛ 13.00–17.00 Wed & Thur, 11.00–17.00 Fri
& Sat ⓝ Tram: 14

Rosentreter Sandra Jahn's collection ranges from suits to new
takes on kilts, caps and hats. She also stocks pieces from the
Paris label Cop. Copine. ⓐ Karl-Heine-Strasse 93 ⓣ 0341 304 1861
ⓦ www.rosentreter-modedesign.de ⓛ 12.00–20.00 Mon–Fri
ⓝ Tram: 14

TAKING A BREAK

Glashaus £ ❶ Surrounded by greenery, this café is the perfect spot to put your feet up after a long stroll in Clara-Zetkin-Park. Take a pew in the leafy beer garden or conservatory to enjoy a cappuccino, beer or ice cream. The restaurant is wheelchair accessible. ⓐ Clara-Zetkin-Park ❶ 0341 962 7873 ⓦ www.glashaus-leipzig.de ⓛ 08.00–late ⓝ Tram: 1

Grüne Tomaten £ ❷ Crammed with memorabilia from the cult film *Fried Green Tomatoes*, this cosy café is a find, not least on account of its warm welcome. The rustic décor includes a gramophone, velvet cushions and baskets suspended from the ceiling. ⓐ Härtelstrasse 27 ❶ 0341 583 2548 ⓛ 09.00–late Mon–Sat ⓝ Tram: 10, 11a

Kowalski Café £ ❸ Arty types and music students hang out in this laid-back, bistro-style café glammed up with a dark wood floor and deep red walls. The counter is full of tempting cakes, which you can savour with a coffee on the terrace. ⓐ Ferdinand-Rhode-Strasse 12 ❶ 0341 212 6020 ⓦ www.das-kowalski.de ⓛ 09.00–01.00 ⓝ Tram: 11

Suppa Summarum £ ❹ Relax on the cushion-lined benches to study the impressive soup menu at this café: choices range from carrot and mandarin to spicy fish from Sierra Leone. If you're still peckish, munch on a feta, peach and strawberry salad, washed down with an apple-and-mint cocktail. If you're still hungry, go on a Wednesday, when it's all-you-can-eat day. ⓐ Münzgasse 16

MESSING ABOUT ON THE RIVER

Nicknamed Little Venice, the river and canals flowing through Plagwitz reveal a different side to Leipzig. Explore the web of waterways by hiring a rowing boat or letting someone else do the hard work. The trip passes natural and industrial landscapes – look up to spy towering plane trees and lofty chimneys.

Those feeling active can rent canoes from the boathouse (❷ Klingerweg 2) or join a three-hour rafting tour departing from Paulis Caféteria (❸ Könneritzstrasse 14). If a lazy cruise sounds more appealing, head for Ristorante Da Vito (❸ Nonnenstrasse 11), where the Italian owner has gone to the pains of importing real Venetian gondolas to shuttle passengers along the White Elster River. For more details, contact the tourist office. ❸ Richard-Wagner-Strasse 1 ❶ 0341 710 4265 ⓦ www.leipzig.de ⓒ 10.00–18.00 Mon–Fri, 09.00–16.00 Sat & Sun

⬥ Cruising for pleasure on the White Elster River

📞 0341 149 4974 🌐 www.suppe-leipzig.de 🕐 11.30–00.00 Mon–Fri, 17.00–00.00 Sat 🚊 Tram:10

Südbrause £–££ ⑤ This rustic café serves up a delicious menu of Italian-inspired dishes. From tagliatelle with salmon, spinach, cherry tomatoes and sunflower seeds to glazed pears with thyme and goats' cheese, there'll be something to whet your appetite. 📍 Karl-Liebknecht-Strasse 154 📞 0341 391 0181 🕐 09.00–late Mon–Fri, 10.00–late Sat & Sun 🚊 Tram: 11

AFTER DARK

RESTAURANTS

Bayerischer Bahnhof £ ⑥ History seeps from every pore of this 19th-century former railway terminus. Today the brewery churns out litres of the famous *Gose* beer. Quench your thirst in the huge, shaded beer garden, or feast on roast pork in ale beside shiny brass boilers in the wood-panelled restaurant. 📍 Bayerischer Platz 1 📞 0341 124 5760 🌐 www.bayerischer-bahnhof.de 🕐 09.00–01.00 🚊 Tram:16

Beirut Night £ ⑦ Rich colours and Lebanese food tempt at this little restaurant on Münzgasse. Dishes like *falafel* (chickpea balls), *halloumi* (fried cheese) and honey-drenched *baklava* are on the menu alongside a selection of water pipes – if you are into *shisha* you can choose from rose, mango and peppermint. 📍 Münzgasse 7 📞 0341 962 8288 🌐 www.restaurantbeirut-night.de 🕐 17.00–00.00 Tues–Sun 🚊 Tram: 10, 11

China White £ ❽ This bright and airy restaurant offers flavoursome Chinese fare such as Peking soup, crispy duck and *chop choi*. **ⓐ** Petersssteinweg 17 **ⓣ** 0341 149 1966 **ⓦ** www.chinawhite-cooking.de **ⓛ** 10.00–14.00, 17.00–23.00 Tues–Sun **ⓝ** Tram: 10

Kanal 28 £ ❾ This former tile factory has been resurrected as a funky restaurant, café and cultural centre. Overlooking the Karl-Heine Canal, the red-brick building attracts a boho crowd to its spacious terrace and art gallery. **ⓐ** Am Kanal 28 **ⓣ** 0341 497 2430 **ⓦ** www.kanal-28.de **ⓛ** 11.30–late Tues–Fri, 10.00–late Sat & Sun **ⓝ** Bus: 60, 80; Tram: 8, 15

Pinocchio £ ❿ Specialities from south Tirol to Sicily whet appetites at this cheery Italian restaurant and pizzeria. When the weather warms, enjoy a glass of Chianti beneath the trees on the terrace. **ⓐ** Karl-Heine-Strasse 27 **ⓣ** 0341 480 3856 **ⓦ** www.pinocchio-leipzig.de **ⓛ** 11.00–23.00 **ⓝ** Tram: 1, 2

Piagor ££ ⓫ Mint-green tones, wood floors and a minimalist décor set the scene at this contemporary restaurant, where creative dishes with an emphasis on fresh fish include spicy papaya-melon soup with king prawns, Andalusian octopus and lobster ravioli. **ⓐ** Münzgasse 3 **ⓣ** 0341 149 4778 **ⓦ** www.piagor.de **ⓛ** 11.30–14.30, 18.00–01.00 Mon–Fri, 18.00–01.00 Sat & Sun **ⓝ** Tram: 10

BARS & CLUBS
La Boum Step into the '80s in this hip bar with its colourfully stylised walls and DJs playing just the right tunes to take you back to the days when the synth was king and the line between

naff and cool was gloriously blurred. Karl-Liebknecht-Strasse 43
 0341 149 4221 11.00–late Mon–Fri, 10.00–late Sat & Sun
 Tram: 10, 11

Distillery If you're into electronic and hip hop beats, this is
one of the best options for catching German and international
DJs and live acts. On Friday it's club night, featuring everything
from breakbeat and drum 'n' bass to hip hop, reggae and
dancehall. Saturdays rave along to techno, house and electro.
 Kurt-Eisner-Strasse 4 0341 3559 7400 www.distillery.de
 23.30–late Fri, 23.00–late Sat Tram: 10, 11

Duke Bar This comfortable and stylish bar is a cool place to
chill out, sip on a cocktail and hang out with the locals and
backpackers from the hostel next door. Every Friday night
there's a party with DJs mixing up everything from electro
to Balkan techno. Riemannstrasse 52 0176 7550 3264
 www.myspace.com/dukeleipzig 10.00–late Tram: 11

Flower Power 'Hippies always welcome' proclaims the
legend, and you get the feeling they really mean it, man. Love,
peace and rock 'n' roll rule in this spit-and-sawdust pub. The
colours are psychedelic, drinks cheap and vibe very mellow.
 Riemannstrasse 42 0341 961 3441 www.flowerpower.eu
 19.00–late Tram: 10, 11

Gastspielhaus This snug, unassuming pub might look like any
other until you step inside and see the walls lined with board
games instead of beer glasses – there are over 500. So if you fancy

a quick game of *Bluff* or want to while away the hours over chess and cheap beer, taking easy euros from locals you've weakened with chasers, this popular haunt is the place to come. ⓐ Peterssteinweg 10 ⓣ 0341 149 7707 ⓦ www.gastspielhaus.de ⓛ 14.00–02.00 Mon–Fri, 10.00–02.00 Sat & Sun ⓝ Tram: 10, 11

Havana Hips sway to sultry Latino tunes at this Cuban club. DJs keep the dance floor packed playing salsa, *merengue* and *cumbia* rhythms. If you've got two left feet come early in the evening to take pointers from the experts at the dance classes. ⓐ Karl-Liebknecht-Strasse 10 ⓣ 0178 557 1361 ⓦ www.havana-leipzig.de ⓛ 20.00–late Wed–Sat ⓝ Tram: 10, 11

Kleine Träumerei Relax in the comfy couches and soak up the local Leipzig atmosphere in this fabulously funky bar. ⓐ Münzgasse 7 ⓣ 0341 2254 0411 ⓦ www.kleine-traeumerei.de ⓛ 11.00–late ⓝ Tram: 10, 11

Stäv Put your beer goggles on to drink Cologne's favourite tipple, gold-hued *Kölsch*, at this relaxed pub doubling as a restaurant. The walls are smothered in photos of some of the luminaries and politicians that have shaped Leipzig's history since 1945. ⓐ Peterssteinweg 10 ⓣ 0341 149 3366 ⓦ www.staev-leipzig.de ⓛ 10.00–late ⓝ Tram: 10, 11

Gohlis & Zoo

Greenery, *Gose* and goals drive most visitors to venture north
of the centre. Culture and commerce have also made their mark
here – grand merchant villas and stately art-nouveau homes
punctuate tree-lined boulevards, once home to wealthy
merchants and fur traders.

SIGHTS & ATTRACTIONS

Aussichtsturm (Rosental Tower)

Rising above a canopy of trees, this 20 m (66 ft) tower crowns
a hill in Rosental Park. It's a bit of a wobbly climb to the top,
but the sweeping views over Leipzig's thick woodlands, canals
and cityscape are well worth the effort. ⓐ Rosental Park
Ⓦ www.leipzig-gohlis.de Ⓝ Tram: 4, 12

Michaeliskirche (St Michael's Church)

Pinned to the centre of Nordplatz, this is one of Leipzig's true
hidden gems. Blending neo-Renaissance, neo-Gothic and art
nouveau styles, the church captivates with its silver-grey
domes, a huge octagonal tower and sublime marble altar.
ⓐ Nordplatz 14 ⓣ 0341 545 509 Ⓦ www.michaelis-friedens.de
Ⓝ Tram: 12

Nordplatz

Admire the tall art nouveau townhouses framing this peaceful
square or relax beside the roses in the tiny, tree-lined park. Look
up to see the bell tower topping the cream-and-terracotta

Leibnizschule Gymnasium school, a striking turn-of-the-century building. ⓝ Tram: 12

Rosental Park

The green lungs of Leipzig, this is an expansive pocket of greenery northwest of the centre. Pathways weave through untamed woodlands and heath on one side and English-style gardens on the other; the park is so big it never feels crowded. Be sure to visit the Blindenpark, a garden that stimulates the senses with touchy-feely plants and scented flowers. There are free open-air barbecue areas near the tower. ⓝ Tram: 3, 4, 7, 12, 16

Waldstrasse Quarter

Slender townhouses with shady inner courtyards cluster in the streets fanning out from Waldstrasse, the epicentre of Leipzig's *Jugendstil* (art nouveau) movement. Many of these imposing 19th-century houses have been restored to their former glory. ⓐ Waldstrasse ⓝ Tram: 4

Zentralstadion Leipzig (Leipzig Central Stadium)

A cool €85 million was spent on creating Leipzig's state-of-the-art stadium in time for the FIFA World Cup 2006. The gigantic steel-and-glass structure forms a perfect oval, accommodating up to 45,000 fans, and boasts the latest technology. A must for football freaks, the venue also hosts a wide range of other sporting events and concerts. If you want to catch a game here, it's wise to book tickets well in advance, as they are in great demand. ⓐ Am Sportforum 2–3 ⓣ Ticket office: 0341 234 1100 ⓦ www.sportforum-leipzig.de

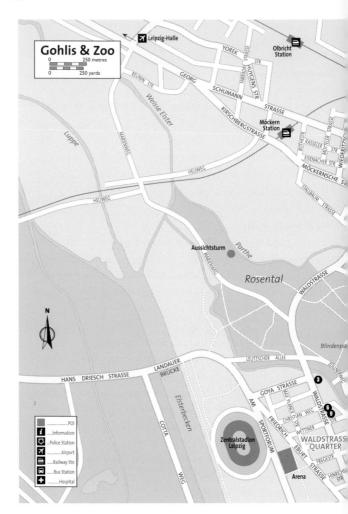

Gohlis & Zoo

0 —————— 250 metres
0 —————— 250 yards

Leipzig-Halle

Olbricht Station

Möckern Station

Aussichtsturm

Rosental

Zentralstadion Leipzig

Arena

WALDSTRASS QUARTER

...POI
...Information
...Police Station
...Airport
...Railway Stn
...Bus Station
...Hospital

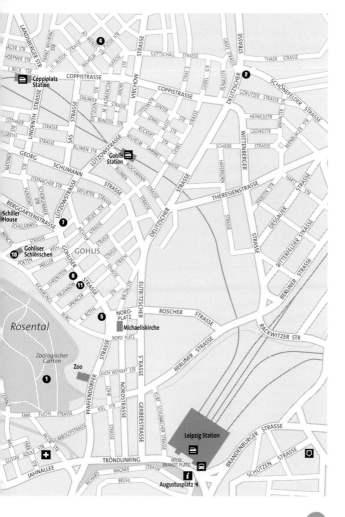

Zoo

A magnet for families, Leipzig's zoo is undergoing an extensive and ambitious renovation programme that's due for completion in 2014. Improvements include the creation of six themed worlds and will massively increase the enclosure sizes and habitats for many animals. The elephant enclosure now provides its larger herd with much-needed space, and for visitors there's an underwater window where you can watch the elephants swim. For kids there's a petting zoo, face painting and an adventure playground. ⓐ Pfaffendorfer Strasse 29 ⓣ 0341 593 3385 ⓦ www.zooleipzig.de ⓛ 09.00–18.00 Apr, Oct; 09.00–17.00 Nov–Mar; 09.00–19.00 May–Sept ⓝ Tram: 12, 16. Admission charge

CULTURE

Arena

Just a few paces from the stadium, this bright and modern arena reels in the crowds with an eclectic programme. Playing host to major sporting events, concerts, galas and conventions, the venue has space for up to 12,000 people and stages everything from glittering West End musicals and Holiday on Ice spectacles to volleyball and tennis championships. ⓐ Am Sportforum 1 ⓣ Ticket hotline: 0341 234 1100 ⓦ www.sportforum-leipzig.de ⓛ Box office: 10.00–19.00 Mon–Fri, 10.00–16.00 Sat ⓝ Tram: 3, 4, 8, 15

Gohliser Schlösschen (Gohlis Palace)

Built for prosperous merchant Caspar Richter in 1756, this sumptuous rococo residence stages cultural events and is a great setting for opera, theatre and classical music. Inside

⬥ *The sumptuous rococo glamour of Gohlis Palace*

glimpse the Oesersaal's elaborate frescoes and the Steinsaal's vaulted ceilings. ⓐ Menckestrasse 23 ⓣ 0341 589 690 ⓦ www.stadtgeschichtliches-museum-leipzig.de ⓛ 10.00–18.00 Tues–Sun, Apr–Oct; 10.00–16.00 Wed–Sun, Nov–Mar ⓜ Tram: 4, 12

Schiller House

Explore this whitewashed 18th-century farmhouse, where famous poet, philosopher and dramatist Friedrich Schiller lived in 1785, and was inspired to pen 'An die Freude' (Ode to Joy), and which houses a small collection of paintings and letters, plus

⬥ Schiller's 18th-century home

Schiller's silk waistcoat. You can catch an open-air concert here in summer. ⓐ Menckestrasse 42 ⓣ 0341 566 2170 ⓦ www.leipzig-gohlis.de/schillerhaus ⓛ 10.00–18.00 summer, 10.00–16.00 Wed–Sun winter ⓝ Tram: 4, 12. Admission charge

RETAIL THERAPY

Natur & Fein Organic is the word on shoppers' lips at this health-conscious store, well stocked with eco-friendly cosmetics, Ayurveda products, fresh fruit and vegetables, locally produced wines, crusty bread, honey – and a tempting antipasti selection in case you're planning a picnic in the park. ⓐ Waldstrasse 23 ⓣ 0341 999 9885 ⓛ 09.00–20.00 Mon–Fri, 09.00–16.00 Sat ⓝ Tram: 4

TAKING A BREAK

Biergarten im Rosental £ ❶ One of the only places you can rest your feet in Rosental Park, this café is conveniently located next to the zoo and has a shady beer garden. Prices are reasonable. ⓐ Pfaffendorfer Strasse 29 ⓣ 0341 583 2503 ⓦ www.zooleipzig.de ⓛ 09.00–19.00 ⓝ Tram. 12, 16

Café Krüger £ ❷ Open 365 days a year, this cosy café has pretty much every homemade cake, flan and pastry you could wish for, from chocolate *Sachertorte* to cherry-rich Black Forest gateau. Forget the diet, it's all far too yummy... ⓐ Delitzscher Strasse 96 ⓣ 0341 911 9145 ⓦ www.cafe-krueger-leipzig.de ⓛ 07.00–22.00 Mon–Fri, 10.00–22.00 Sat & Sun ⓝ Tram: 14, 16

Mücken Schlösschen £ ❸ A huge leafy beer garden overlooks the canal at this castle-like building with turrets and towers. After a long walk in the Rosental, pull up a chair beside the fountain to drink Bavarian *Paulaner* beer and snack on white sausages slathered in mustard. ⓐ Waldstrasse 86 ❶ 0341 983 2051 ⓦ www.mueckenschloesschen-leipzig.de ❶ 11.00–late ⓝ Tram: 4

Sehbrücke Restaurant £ ❹ Join the locals at this friendly gastro-pub offering value-for-money light meals like chilli con carne and goulash, washed down with plenty of bittersweet *Schwarzbier*. ⓐ Wilhelm-Plesse-Strasse 12 ❶ 0341 562 9768 ❶ 17.00–late Mon–Sat, Oct–May; 18.00–late Mon–Sat, June–Sept ⓝ Tram: 12

Sontag & Dünkel £ ❺ This unassuming little bakery opposite St Michael's Church serves a hearty breakfast for around €3 that includes as much tea or coffee as you can drink. ⓐ Nordplatz 7 ❶ 0341 564 7255 ❶ 06.00–18.00 Mon–Fri, 07.00–16.00 Sat, 08.00–16.00 Sun ⓝ Tram: 12

AFTER DARK

RESTAURANTS
Frida la Mexicana £ ❻ Fiery Mexican flavours are on the menu at this restaurant, which is magnificently decked out in bright pinks and blues. As the name suggests, the owner has a penchant for Frida Kahlo's work, and larger-than-life portraits of the artist decorate the walls, looking down on you as you sink your fangs into yet another *quesadilla*. ⓐ Waldstrasse 64 ❶ 0341 308 6477 ⓦ www.frida-la-mexicana.de ❶ 17.00–01.00 Tues–Sun ⓝ Tram: 4

La Locanda £ 7 Savour some (or even a lot) of the well-prepared antipasti, pizza and pasta at this intimate Italian restaurant, which affords some rather lovely views to Friedenskirche church from the attractive terrace. ⓐ Gohliser Strasse 42 ⓣ 0341 689 4745 ⓦ www.la-locanda.com ⓛ 12.00–14.30, 17.30–23.00 Sun–Fri, 17.30–23.30 Sat ⓝ Tram: 12

Ofenrohr £ 8 An inspired choice for al-fresco dining in summer, this laid-back place serves wholesome, fill-your-boots fare like Saxon *Sauerbraten* (beef pot roast) with mounds of red cabbage. If you'd prefer something more international, dishes range from rabbit to lamb curry. ⓐ Gohliser Strasse 13 ⓣ 0341 561 4333 ⓛ 10.00–late ⓝ Tram: 12

Trattoria No 1 £ 9 Hundreds of wine bottles line the shelves at this authentic trattoria, which boasts a cavernous cellar. The design is simple but elegant, and the exquisitely prepared specialities range from seafood linguine to freshly baked pizza. ⓐ Waldstrasse 64 ⓣ 0341 211 7098 ⓛ 12.00–14.30, 18.00–00.00 Mon–Fri, 18.00–00.00 Sat & Sun ⓝ Tram: 4

Gohliser Schlösschen ££ 10 Posh with a capital P, this palatial (with another capital P) restaurant is all cream leather, vaulted ceilings and arched windows. The chef uses seasonal produce to create some truly unforgettable specialities like veal carpaccio in tomato vinaigrette and mascarpone figs with rosemary. ⓐ Menckestrasse 23 ⓣ 0341 561 2992 ⓦ www.gohliser-schloss.de ⓛ 12.00–14.00, 18.00–22.00 Tues–Sun ⓝ Tram: 4, 12

La Mirabelle ££ ⑪ French cuisine is served with finesse in this art-nouveau restaurant. Enjoy fiddling charismatically with mussels in wine or Roquefort *gratin* on the terrace. ⓐ Gohliser Strasse 11 ⓣ 0341 590 2981 ⓦ http://la-mirabelle.de ⓛ 11.30–15.00, 18.00–late Mon–Fri, 19.00–late Sat & Sun ⓝ Tram: 12

BARS

Die Gohliserwirtschaft A terrace shaped like a ship complete with decking, fishing nets and lanterns welcomes you to this nautical-themed pub in summer. In winter take a pew at a chunky wooden table to drink local brews and eat *Leipziger Allerlei* stew. ⓐ Gohliser Strasse 20 ⓣ 0341 564 4033 ⓦ www.gohliser.de ⓛ 11.00–01.00 ⓝ Tram: 12

Gosenschenke Ohne Bedenken Dating back to 1899, this traditional Gosenschenke inn has won a string of awards as one of Germany's best pubs and beer gardens. Oozing musty charm, the wood-panelled cellar serves a long list of *Gose* beer varieties and specialities like *Gose-Häppchen* (pickled Camembert and gherkins) and *Gosebraten* (*Gose*-marinated beef). ⓐ Menckestrasse 5 ⓣ 0341 566 2360 ⓦ www.gosenschenke.de ⓛ 12.00–00.00 ⓝ Tram: 4, 11

Mega Bar Relaxed and unpretentious, this local haunt is a pleasant spot for a quiet beer and snack. The comfortable café-cum-bar doubles as a free Wi-Fi hotspot. ⓐ Gohliser Strasse 19 ⓣ 0341 583 1188 ⓦ www.mega-bar.de ⓛ 09.00–late ⓝ Tram: 12

▲ *Go for a Gose at this traditional inn*

THE GOLDEN *GOSE*

It would be sacrilege to visit Leipzig without trying at least one glass of gold-hued *Gose* beer at a traditional inn like Gosenschenke Ohne Bedenken. This tangy, top-fermented wheat beer takes its name from the *Gose* stream, which flows through the town of Goslar to the west of Leipzig. For a beer with a twist, order a *Sonnenschirm* (parasol) laced with fruit syrup, a *Frauenfreundlicher* (ladies' friend) with a shot of cherry liqueur, or a *Regenschirm* (umbrella) with a dash of *Kümmel* liqueur.

The city's tipple of choice has an intoxicating history, stretching back 1,000 years to when Emperor Otto III sung the beer's praises. In medieval times it was brewed in Goslar and finally came to Leipzig in 1738, where it became the preferred brew of the *Studiosen* (students), among them Goethe and Schiller. Under Communist rule (1949–90), the beer disappeared from the scene.

With a dedicated passion for *Gose*, Dr Harmut Hennebach gave the beer a new lease of life when he reopened Gosenschenke Ohne Bedenken in 1990. Today, the lightly acidic beer is brewed according to a traditional recipe, with coriander and salt, and sold in long-necked bottles. Leipzig legend still has it that a stroll in the Rosental followed by a *Gose* beer (or three) is all you need in life to be happy and healthy.

▶ *Cathedral entrance at Halle bids visitors welcome*

Halle

Handel, Goethe and Martin Luther all waxed lyrical about Halle, a vibrant university city built high on the riches of its 'white gold' – salt. Climbing medieval castles, cruising the River Saale and chilling on the tower-framed market square, it isn't hard to see why.

GETTING THERE

Located 40 km (25 miles) to the northwest of Leipzig, it's easy to reach Halle by public transport. Frequent Deutsche Bahn train connections link the two cities, just half an hour's journey apart. If you're driving, take the A14 motorway.

SIGHTS & ATTRACTIONS

Alter Markt
Hemmed in by half-timbered and Renaissance houses, this square was once home to Halle's wealthy salt merchants. In the centre is the Eselbrunnen (Donkey Fountain).
ⓐ Alter Markt Ⓝ Tram: 2, 5, 7

Boating the River Saale
Hire a canoe or rowing boat to explore the River Saale, or board a 20-km (12^1/$_2$-mile) tour to Wettin. If you're lucky, you'll spot a swamp beaver. ⓐ Riveufer 10 ❶ 0151 1720 9964
Ⓦ www.bootsverleih-wiederhold.de ❹ 11.00–19.00 Apr–Oct
Ⓝ Tram: 7, 8

Botanischer Garten (Botanic Gardens)

The 300-year-old botanic gardens nurture 12,000 species.
🅐 Am Kirchtor 3 📞 0345 552 6271 🌐 www2.biologie.uni-halle.de
🕐 14.00–18.00 Mon–Fri, Apr–Oct 🚋 Tram: 7. Admission charge

Dom (Cathedral)

Originally part of a Dominican monastery, Halle's early Gothic
cathedral impresses with its baroque art and Peter Schro
sculptures. 🅐 Domplatz 📞 0345 202 1359 🌐 www.dom-halle.de
🕐 14.00–16.00 June–Oct 🚋 Tram: 2, 9, 10

Franckesche Stiftung (Francke Foundations)

One of Germany's key cultural landmarks, this vast 17th-century
orphanage comprises 25 institutions including a museum, library
and music school. A must-see is the Cabinet of Curiosities, sheltering
everything from fine art to whale bones. 🅐 Franckeplatz 1
📞 0345 212 7450 🌐 www.francke-halle.de 🕐 10.00–17.00
Tues–Sun 🚋 Tram: 2, 4, 5, 7, 9. Admission charge

Marktkirche (Market Church)

Peer up at the four towers crowning this late Gothic church,
where Martin Luther the Reformer once preached – his death
mask is located in the sacristy. Step inside to admire Renaissance
art and the organ on which Handel played his first notes.
🅐 An der Marienkirche 2 📞 0345 517 0894 🌐 www.marktkirche-
halle.de 🕐 10.00–17.00 Mon–Sat 🚋 Tram: 2, 5, 7, 8, 9, 10

Marktplatz (Market Square)

All streets lead to Halle's huge market square. Glimpse the five

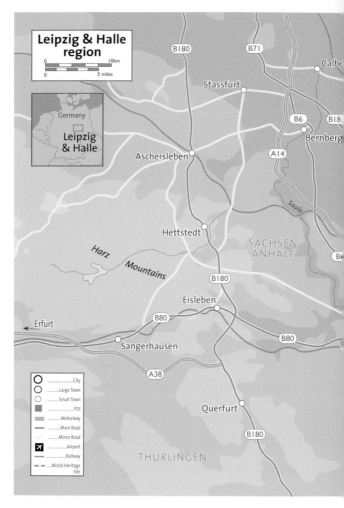

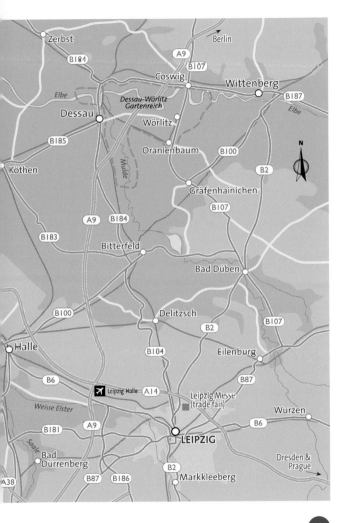

towers dominating the skyline, the bronze Handel monument and the Marktschlösschen's blushing bricks and gables. **a** Marktplatz **N** Tram: 2, 5, 9

Oberburg Giebichenstein (Giebichenstein Castle)

Clinging to rocks above the River Saale, this 10th-century fortress is all silvery turrets and thick curtain walls. Roam the foundations and vaults at the open-air museum. The surrounding parkland affords fine river views. **a** Seebener Strasse 1 **T** 0345 523 3857 **L** 10.00–18.00 Tues–Fri, 10.00–19.00 Sat & Sun, Apr–Oct **N** Tram: 7. Admission charge

CULTURE

Beatles Museum

A shrine to the singing Liverpudlians, this museum is crammed with Beatles memorabilia. **a** Alter Markt 12 **T** 0345 290 3900 **W** www.beatlesmuseum.net **L** 10.00–20.00 Wed–Sun **N** Tram: 2, 5. Admission charge

Kulturinsel (Culture Island)

The eclectic programme at Halle's cultural enclave moves from cutting-edge plays to dancing marionettes. **a** Grosse Ulrichstrasse 50–51 **T** 0345 205 0222 **W** www.kulturinsel-halle.de **N** Tram: 2, 7

Landesmuseum für Vorgeschichte (National Museum for Prehistory)

This fascinating museum houses ten million artefacts that range all the way from dinosaur bones to a primitive man's fossilised remains. The Bronze Age Nebra Sky Disc is the world's oldest chart of the heavens. ⓐ Richard-Wagner-Strasse 9 ❶ 0345 524 730 ⓦ www.lda-lsa.de ⓛ 09.00–19.30 Tues, 09.00–17.00 Wed–Fri, 10.00–18.00 Sat & Sun ⓝ Tram: 7. Admission charge

Opernhaus Halle (Opera House)

Halle's neoclassical opera house stages opera, operetta, ballet, musicals and cabaret. ⓐ Universitätsring 24 ❶ 0345 51100 ⓦ www.opernhaus- halle.de ⓛ Ticket office: 10.00–20.00 Mon–Sat ⓝ Tram: 1, 2, 5, 7, 9

Stiftung Moritzburg: Kunstmuseum des Landes Sachsen-Anhalt (Moritzburg Art Gallery)

Sitting on 500 years of history, this red-turreted castle showcases 19th- and 20th-century artworks. Keep an eye open for Expressionist works by Otto Mueller and Edvard Munch. ⓐ Friedemann-Bach-Platz 5 ❶ 0345 212 590 ⓦ www.kunstmuseum-moritzburg.de ⓛ 11.00–20.30 Tues, 10.00–18.00 Wed–Sun ⓝ Tram: 1, 2, 5, 7, 9. Admission charge

Technisches Halloren- und Salinemuseum (Technical Saltworks Museum)

Housed in a beautiful half-timbered building, this former Prussian saltworks traces Halle's history, with demonstrations and displays of original costumes and equipment. ⓐ Mansfelder Strasse 52 ❶ 0345 209 3230 ⓦ www.mv-sachsen-anhalt.de ⓛ 10.00–17.00 Tues–Sun ⓝ Tram: 4, 9. Admission charge

TAKING A BREAK

Bücher-Café La Lit £ Warm terracotta tones and squishy sofas give this café on the market square a relaxed feel. ⓐ Marktplatz 3 ⓣ 0345 293 7202 ⓛ 09.30–20.00 Mon–Fri, 09.30–18.00 Sat ⓝ Tram: 2, 5

Café Schade £ Baked according to a centuries-old family recipe, the cakes at this 400-year-old patisserie near the river make mouths water. ⓐ Seebener Strasse 20 ⓣ 0345 523 1551 ⓛ 09.00–18.00 Mon–Sat, 10.00–18.00 Sun ⓝ Tram: 8, 12

Eiscafe Florenz £ Floor-to-ceiling glass lets light flood into this Italian café. ⓐ Leipziger Chaussee 147 ⓣ 0345 688 8902 ⓛ 09.00–20.00 Mon–Sat, 14.00–18.00 Sun ⓝ Bus: 43

Il Rospo £ Chocoholics indulge their cravings at this tiny café which prides itself on using organic, seasonal ingredients. ⓐ Burgstrasse 4 ⓣ 0345 682 4464 ⓦ www.ilrospo.de ⓛ 10.00–22.00 Tues–Sat, 10.00–18.00 Sun ⓝ Tram: 7

Krug zum Grünen Kranze £ This riverside café has entrancing views of Giebichenstein Castle. ⓐ Talstrasse 37 ⓣ 0345 299 8899 ⓦ www.krugzumgruenenkranze.de ⓛ 11.00–late ⓝ Tram: 7

AFTER DARK

RESTAURANTS
Matador £ This authentic Argentinian restaurant serves prime,

incisor-tempting Black Angus beef. Be sure to try the South American speciality, *matambre* (beef strips, corn and pumpkin). ⓐ Geiststrasse 32 ⓣ 0345 678 4443 ⓦ www.steakhaus-matador.de ⓛ 17.00–23.00 ⓝ Tram: 3, 7, 8, 10

Mönchshof £ Beamed ceilings and murals set the scene in this Hallemarkt restaurant. The terrace has views of the Göbel-Brunnen fountain. ⓐ Talamtstrasse 6 ⓣ 0345 202 1726 ⓦ www.moenchshof-halle.de ⓛ 11.00–late Mon–Sat, 11.00–15.00 Sun ⓝ Tram: 2, 5, 9

PalaisS £ Whether you fancy a spicy stir-fry, sausage salad or seafood paella, this beautiful red-brick restaurant with riverside terrace comes up with the goods. ⓐ Ankerstrasse 3c ⓣ 0345 977 2651 ⓦ www.palaiss.de ⓛ 18.00–late Mon–Sat, 10.00–late Sun ⓝ Tram: 2, 9

Sushi am Opernhaus £ The décor is minimalistic, the ingredients fresh and the clientele laid back in this Japanese restaurant. ⓐ August-Bebel-Strasse 3–5 ⓣ 0345 681 6627 ⓦ www.sushifreunde.de ⓛ 11.30–14.00, 18.00–22.00 Mon–Fri, 18.00–23.00 Sat, 18.00–22.00 Sun ⓝ Tram: 2, 5, 7

Zum Ritter £ Go back to medieval times at this castle-like restaurant, where you can grill skewered kebabs over hot lava stones and drink *steins* of beer as folk music plays. ⓐ Sternstrasse 7 ⓣ 0345 294 3027 ⓛ 11.30–00.00 Sat, 17.00–00.00 Sun & Mon ⓝ Tram: 2, 5

Zur Schnitzelwirtin £ Sunny yellow walls and 70 different kinds of *Schnitzel* make this a top choice for carnivores with big appetites. ⓐ Grosse Märkerstrasse 18 ⓣ 0345 202 9938 ⓦ www.schnitzelwirtin.de ⓛ 11.30–23.00 Mon–Sat, 11.00–15.00 Sun ⓝ Tram: 2, 5

BARS & CLUBS

Enchilada Halle's party people head here for jumbo margarita cocktails, tequila shots and Mexican beer. Happy hour is from 18.00 to 21.00. ⓐ Universitätsring 6 ⓣ 0345 686 7755 ⓦ www.enchilada.de ⓛ 18.00–02.00 ⓝ Tram: 7

Mo's Daniels Metrosexuals sink into the chocolate-brown leather sofas at this sleek café-cum-bar serving late-night snacks. ⓐ Bernburgerstrasse 1 ⓣ 0345 686 9800 ⓦ www.mosdaniels.de ⓛ 19.00–03.30 ⓝ Tram: 8

Turm Set in Moritzburg's stone ramparts, this club hosts some of Halle's hottest parties. from rock bands to poetry slams. But there's a little something for everyone in between, such as gay dance parties to African disco or gothic-industrial nights. Be sure to check the website for programme details. ⓐ Friedemann-Bach-Platz 5 ⓣ 0345 458 4686 ⓛ 11.00–late Mon–Fri, 18.00–late Sat & Sun

Zanzibar This popular haunt's alcoholic smoothies – Mocha Orange and French Connection, for instance – take some beating. ⓐ Universitätsring 6a ⓣ 0345 686 7420 ⓦ www.zanzi-bar.de ⓛ 11.00–late Mon–Fri, 16.00–late Sat & Sun ⓝ Tram: 7

ACCOMMODATION

Jugendherberge Halle £ Near the Opera House, this central youth hostel offers the cheapest digs in town. Located in a pretty villa, dorms are spacious and clean. **ⓐ** August-Bebel-Strasse 48a **ⓣ** 0345 202 4716 **ⓦ** www.jugendherberge.de **ⓝ** Tram: 2, 5

City-Hotel am Wasserturm ££ The modern, light-flooded rooms at this peaceful hotel are a good base for exploring the banks of the River Saale by bike or on foot. **ⓐ** Lessingstrasse 8 **ⓣ** 0345 29820 **ⓦ** www.cityhotel-halle.de **ⓝ** Tram: 12

Dormotel Halle ££ Near the main station, this hotel offers contemporary rooms. Enjoy breakfast in the frescoed dining room or on the terrace. **ⓐ** Delitzscher Strasse 17 **ⓣ** 0345 57120 **ⓦ** www.dormotel-halle.de **ⓝ** Tram: 7, 9

Galerie Hotel Esprit ££ Expect a warm welcome and personalised service at this arty hotel. The 19th-century terracotta-coloured house doubles as a gallery, staging regular exhibitions. **ⓐ** Torstrasse 7 **ⓣ** 0345 212 200 **ⓦ** www.esprit-hotel.de **ⓝ** Bus: 27

Hotel Am Ratshof ££ This whitewashed townhouse near the market square features a 15th-century vaulted cellar and leafy beer garden. Spacious rooms have comfy beds and a hearty breakfast is included in the price. **ⓐ** Rathausstrasse 14 **ⓣ** 0345 202 5632 **ⓦ** www.hotel-am-ratshof.de **ⓝ** Tram: 1, 2

Dessau-Wörlitz Gartenreich

In this UNESCO World Heritage Site, you can be spotting beavers by the lake one minute and sipping B52s in a trendy bar the next. Welcome to a wilderness with an urban edge.

GETTING THERE

The speedy A14 and A9 motorways link Leipzig to the Dessau-Wörlitz Gartenreich, a 50-minute drive away. There are good and frequent Deutsche Bahn train connections to Dessau. If you're travelling to Wörlitz, take bus number 333 from Dessau's bus station.

SIGHTS & ATTRACTIONS

Bauhaus Dessau

An awesome block of concrete, glass and steel designed by Bauhaus director Walter Gropius, this is a prime example of the kind of creations that emanated from the German art school in the 1920s. Each space is designed differently, so allow time to take in the whole building. ⓐ Gropiusallee 38 ⓣ 0340 65080 ⓦ www.bauhaus-dessau.de ⓛ 10.00–18.00 ⓝ Bus: 10, 11. Admission charge

Fürst Franz Weg (Fürst Franz Path)

Hire your own set of wheels from Dessau's main station to pedal this 60-km (37 1/2-mile) trail slicing through the Gartenreich. Flitting from one palace and garden to the next, pause to explore Grosskühnau and Georgium. ⓐ Mobilitätszentrale der DVV-

Stadtwerke Dessau at the Hauptbahnhof, Dessau ☎ 0340 213 366
🕐 09.00–17.00

Gotisches Haus

With its turrets, towers and peaches-and-cream interior, this
neo-Gothic mansion is the architectural equivalent of a wedding
cake. Watch the light hit the Rittersaal's magnificent stained-
glass windows or come in the evening to see them illuminated.
ⓐ Wörlitz ⓦ www.gartenreich.com 🕐 10.00–18.00 Tues–Sun,
May–Sept; 10.00–17.00 Sat & Sun, Apr & Oct ⓝ Bus: 333.
Admission charge

Grosskühnau

Retreat to this English-inspired landscape garden and reed-
fringed nature reserve, hugging the banks of Lake Kühnau.
Picnic beside gentle slopes of vines and catch a glimpse of
Giacobo Pozzi's Italian-designed Vineyard House – a snippet
of Tuscany in Saxony-Anhalt! ⓐ Schloss Grosskühnau, Dessau
☎ 0340 646 150 ⓦ www.gartenreich.com ⓝ Bus: 10, 11

Lake Wörlitz

Swap Venice for Wörlitz's shimmering lake and canals aboard a
brightly painted gondola. The 45-minute tour takes in highlights
such as the Gotisches Haus. ⓐ Gondola Station ☎ 0349 052 0205
🕐 10.00–18.00, May–Sept; 11.00–16.00, Oct–Apr ⓝ Bus: 333

Luisium

Surrounded by open countryside, Luisium Palace fuses Classical
and neo-Gothic elements. Take a peek at the banqueting hall's

murals, then relax in the flower-strewn gardens. ⓐ Schloss
Luisium, Dessau ⓣ 0340 218 3711 ⓦ www.gartenreich.com
ⓛ 10.00–17.00 Tues–Sun, Apr & Oct; 10.00–18.00 Tues–Sun,
May–Sept ⓝ Bus: 13. Admission charge

Meisterhäuser (Masters' Houses)

These cube-shaped houses are where Bauhaus masters
like Walter Gropius, Oskar Schlemmer, Wassily Kandinsky
and Paul Klee once lived and worked. A highlight is the
colourful Kandinsky/Klee House, where the walls are painted
170 different shades. ⓐ Ebertallee, Dessau ⓣ 0340 661 0934
ⓦ www.meisterhaeuser.de ⓛ 10.00–18.00 Tues–Sun, Feb–Oct;
10.00–17.00 Tues–Sun, Nov–Jan ⓝ Bus: 10, 11. Admission charge

◗ *Take to the water at Lake Wörlitz*

Middle Elbe Biosphere Reserve

This expansive floodplain forest beckons nature lovers. Hiking or biking, you'll pass half-moon lakes, woodlands and meadows. But the big draw is the endangered beaver. The beaver enclosure observation deck is the best place to spot them. The Auenhaus information centre provides more details. ⓐ Auenhaus, Dessau ⓣ 0349 044 0610 ⓦ www.biosphaerenreservatmittlereelbe.de ⓛ Info Centre Auenhaus: 10.00–16.00 Tues-Fri, 10.00–17.00 Sat & Sun, May–Oct; 10.00–16.00 Nov–Apr; beaver compound: 11.00–17.00 Sat & Sun, May–Oct ⓝ Bus: 331

Oranienbaum

Sniff out fragrant citrus trees in Europe's longest orangery. A highlight is the Chinese garden with its octagonal pagoda

> **CALLING CULTURE VULTURES …**
> The best way to discover compact Dessau is to walk the
> Culture Trail, taking in Dessau's key sights such as the
> Bauhaus, Anhalt Theatre, Georgium Palace and the neo-
> Renaissance town hall. The bronze signs on the pavement
> will help you find your way. The **tourist office** (ⓐ Zerbster
> Strasse 2c ① 0340 204 1442 Ⓦ www.dessau.de) provides
> free maps.

and stone bridges. The baroque palace shelters Dutch treasures
from tapestries to blue-and-white ceramics. ⓐ Oranienbaum
① 0349 042 0259 Ⓦ www.oranienbaum.de ⓒ Museum:
11.00–17.00 Tues–Sun, Apr & Oct; 10.00–18.00 Tues–Sun,
May–Sept ⓝ Bus: 331, 333. Admission charge

Schloss Mosigkau (Mosigkau Palace)
Princess Anna Wilhelmine of Anhalt-Dessau poured pots of
her daddy's money into building this sublime rococo palace,
adorned with Rubens paintings and baroque furniture, and
complete with a mind-boggling maze. ⓐ Knobelsdorffallee 2/2,
Dessau ① 0340 521 139 Ⓦ www.gartenreich.com ⓒ 10.00–18.00
Tues–Sun, Apr–Oct ⓝ Bus: 16; Tram: 3. Admission charge

Schloss Wörlitz (Wörlitz Palace)
This grand 18th-century palace was the summer residence
of Prince Leopold III. His royal jewels include Rubens originals
and English ceramics. The palace overlooks the mirror-like Lake

Wörlitz. **ⓐ** Wörlitz **ⓣ** 0349 052 0302 **ⓦ** www.gartenreich.com
ⓛ 10.00–17.00 Tues–Sun, Apr & Oct; 10.00–18.00 Tues–Sun,
May–Sept **ⓝ** Bus: 333. Admission charge

Tierpark Dessau
Come eye-to-eye with brown bears and alpacas at Dessau's
zoo, set in leafy grounds near the station. **ⓐ** Querallee 8,
Dessau **ⓣ** 0340 614 426 **ⓦ** www.tierpark.dessau.de
ⓛ 09.00–18.00 summer; 09.00–dusk winter **ⓝ** Train:
Hauptbahnhof. Admission charge

▲ *Rococo rapture at Schloss Mosigkau*

CULTURE

Anhalt Theatre

Dessau's columned theatre stages philharmonic orchestra performances, opera, operettas, musicals, plays, ballet and puppet theatre for younger audiences. ⓐ Friedensplatz 1A, Dessau ⓣ 0340 2511 333 ⓦ www.anhaltisches-theater.de ⓛ 10.00–17.00 Mon–Fri ⓝ Tram: 1, 3

Georgium (Anhalt Art Gallery)

A stroll through these sculpture-dotted landscape gardens on the River Elbe's banks leads to the Anhalt Art Gallery, housed in Georgium Palace. The picture gallery's 2,000-strong collection includes masterpieces by Dutch and Flemish Masters. ⓐ Puschkinallee 100, Dessau ⓣ 0340 6612 6000 ⓦ www.georgium.de ⓛ 10.00–17.00 Tues–Sun ⓝ Bus: 10, 11. Admission charge

RETAIL THERAPY

Galerie Bauart Take home your own bit of Bauhaus from Dessau's interior design gallery: there are some nifty design knick-knacks that won't break the bank. ⓐ Gropiusallee 81, Dessau ⓣ 0340 661 0246 ⓦ www.galerie-bauart.de ⓛ 12.00–18.00 Fri, Sat & Sun ⓝ Bus: 10, 11

Hofladen An obligatory picnic stop, this shop is crammed with locally sourced organic produce like freshly pressed apple juice, mustards, honey, sausages and creamy goats'

cheese. ⓐ Pötnitz 6, Dessau-Mildensee ⓣ 0340 21940
ⓦ www.mildenseer-hofladen.de ⓛ 09.00–18.00 Tues–Fri,
09.00–12.00 Sat

TAKING A BREAK

Gastwirtschaft im Küchengebäude £ Right next to Wörlitz
Palace, munch on spit-roasted wild boar by an open fire
or sip beer on the cobbled terrace. ⓐ Am Wörlitzer Schloss
ⓣ 0349 052 2338 ⓛ 11.00–18.00 Mon, 11.00–21.00 Tues–Thur
& Sun, 11.00–21.30 Fri, 11.00–22.00 Sat ⓝ Bus: 333

⬥ The royal palace of Wörlitz

Klub im Bauhaus £ Take a bite out of Bauhaus at this shrine to 1920s design. Nibble pastries with an espresso on white plastic stools or enjoy tapas with a nice glass of red on the terrace. ⓐ Gropiusallee 38, Dessau ⓣ 0340 650 8444 ⓦ www.klubimbauhaus.de ⓛ 09.00–00.00 ⓝ Bus: 10, 11

Moni's Konditorei und Cafe £ Sticky pastries and delicious handmade cakes forbid you to count calories at this snug café. ⓐ Neue Reihe 179, Wörlitz ⓣ 0349 052 0124 ⓦ www.monis-konditorei.de ⓛ 10.00–17.00 Mon–Sat, 14.00–17.00 Sun ⓝ Bus: 333

AFTER DARK

RESTAURANTS
Brauhaus zum Alten Dessauer £ The menu is meaty at this wood-beamed brewery and beer garden. Feast on roast pork knuckles with a glass of amber-hued *Alter Dessauer* beer. ⓐ Lange Gasse 16, Dessau ⓣ 0340 220 5909 ⓦ www.alter-dessauer.de ⓛ 11.00–00.00 ⓝ Tram: 1, 2

Kartoffelkäfer £ From fiery Hungarian potato soup to Peruvian potato stew, this place gives culinary credit to the humble potato. ⓐ Neue Reihe 149, Wörlitz ⓣ 0349 052 0509 ⓦ www.kartoffelkaefer-woerlitz.de ⓛ 12.00–22.00 ⓝ Bus: 333

Kornhaus Restaurant £ Soak up River Elbe views through the glass windows of this sphere-shaped Bauhaus restaurant, where a granary once stood. ⓐ Kornhausstrasse 146, Dessau

☎ 0340 640 4141 **Ⓦ** www.kornhaus.de **🕒** 11.00–23.00 Fri–Wed
Ⓝ Bus: 10, 11

Tokyo Haus ££ Sushi fans tuck into well-prepared fish and vegetarian specialities at this contemporary Japanese restaurant. **ⓐ** Elisabethstrasse 41, Dessau **☎** 0340 661 5918 **Ⓦ** www.tokyo-haus.de **🕒** 11.30–14.30, 17.00–23.00 Tues–Fri, 12.00–23.00 Sat & Sun **Ⓝ** Tram: 1, 3

BARS & CLUBS

Chaplin's A head-spinning cocktail list, mellow grooves and cheap prices tempt at this New York-style bar. **ⓐ** Wolfgangstrasse 14, Dessau **☎** 0340 220 0444 **Ⓦ** www.starsdiner.de **🕒** 18.00–late Mon–Fri, 14.00–late Sat & Sun **Ⓝ** Tram: 3

Cup & Cino Serving Dessau's frothiest cappuccino and freshest salads, this Italian-style café transforms into a funky bar by night, where DJs spin lounge music. **ⓐ** Zerbster Strasse 30, Dessau **☎** 0340 250 8869 **Ⓦ** www.cupcino.com **🕒** 09.00–late Mon–Fri, 10.00–late Sat & Sun **Ⓝ** Tram: 1, 2

Kiez Café Drawing a young crowd, this chilled café stages plenty of events. Happy hour is from 20.00 to 22.00. **ⓐ** Bertolt-Brecht-Strasse 29, Dessau **☎** 0340 212 032 **Ⓦ** www.kiez-ev.de/cafe **🕒** 19.00–00.00 Mon–Fri, 19.00–02.00 Sat **Ⓝ** Tram: 1

Projekt 1 Come here to relax with cocktails on the black-and-cream leather benches. **ⓐ** Zerbster Strasse 2, Dessau **☎** 0340 230 1230 **Ⓦ** www.projekt-eins.de **🕒** 18.00–late **Ⓝ** Tram: 1

ACCOMMODATION

Adria £ A sound choice for water babies and the budget conscious, this lakeside campsite has spacious, shady pitches right beside Lake Mildensee. There's an on-site bistro, barbecue area, laundry and playground. **ⓐ** Campingplatz 'Adria', Dessau-Mildensee **ⓣ** 0340 230 4810 **ⓦ** www.cuct.de **ⓝ** Bus: Strandbad Adria

Heuhotel £ For back-to-nature fun, head for Wörlitz's hay hotel. This wood-beamed barn is full to the brim with lovely soft hay, where you'll sleep sweetly and very cheaply. You can rent a sleeping bag for a couple of euros. **ⓐ** Neue Reihe 149, Wörlitz **ⓣ** 0349 052 0509 **ⓦ** www.kartoffelkaefer-woerlitz.de **ⓝ** Bus: 333

Jugendherberge Dessau £ Directly on the Elbe cycling trail, this Dessau youth hostel is surrounded by trees. The excellent facilities include a terrace, table tennis, basketball and bike hire. Comfy beds will soothe those cycling muscles. **ⓐ** Waldkaterweg 11, Dessau **ⓣ** 0340 619 452 **ⓦ** www.jugendherberge.de **ⓝ** Bus: 10, 11

Zum Hauenden Schwein ££ Recently renovated from top to bottom, this hotel has bags of character. The rooms evoke a country cottage with floral prints and squishy beds. **ⓐ** Erdmannsdorffstrasse 69, Wörlitz **ⓣ** 0349 053 0190 **ⓦ** www.pension-zum-hauenden-schwein.de **ⓝ** Bus: 333

ⓞ *The Leipzig tourist information centre*

PRACTICAL information

Directory

GETTING THERE
By air
A number of airlines operate a frequent, direct service between Leipzig-Halle Airport and 60 European destinations including London, Paris and Vienna. A 20-minute journey from the centre of Leipzig, the modern airport offers a full range of services.
Air Berlin ⓦ www.airberlin.com
Germanwings ⓦ www.germanwings.com

Many people are aware that air travel emits CO_2, which contributes to climate change. You may be interested in the possibility of lessening the environmental impact of your flight through the charity **Climate Care** (ⓦ www.climatecare.org), which offsets your CO_2 by funding environmental projects around the world.

By rail
Leipzig's gleaming main station has excellent connections on high-speed ICE trains to major German cities including Berlin, Frankfurt, Munich and Hamburg. **Deutsche Bahn** (ⓦ www.bahn.de) provides information on routes and timetables.

By road
Germany's roads are well maintained, although the lack of a speed limit on motorways means it can get a bit fast and furious at times. Driving is on the right. If possible, it's wise to avoid morning and evening rush hours (07.30–09.00 and 16.00–18.00).

National Express (Ⓦ www.nationalexpress.com) and **Eurolines** (Ⓦ www.eurolines.com) operate a Europe-wide service and pull into Leipzig's main bus station in front of the main train station.

ENTRY FORMALITIES

EU, Australian, Canadian, New Zealand and United States citizens must have a valid passport to enter Germany, but do not require a visa for stays of less than 90 days. If you are arriving from another country, you may need a visa and should contact your consulate or embassy before departure. The German Embassy provides more information on entry requirements at Ⓦ www.auswaertiges-amt.de

It is free to import goods worth up to €175 from a non-EU country, but you should check restrictions on the imports of tobacco, perfume and alcohol. Further information is available from the German customs website Ⓦ www.zoll.de

MONEY

The national currency is the euro (€), broken down into 100 cents. Coins are in denominations of 1, 2, 5, 10, 20 and 50 cents, and of 1 and 2 euro. There are banknotes of 5, 10, 20, 50, 100, 200 and 500 euro.

There are plenty of ATMs in Leipzig and the surrounding areas where you can withdraw cash with a credit card 24 hours a day. Banks are normally open 09.00–18.00 from Monday to Thursday and 09.30–16.00 on Friday. Main branches like Deutsche Bank on Augustsplatz do not close for lunch.

You'll find bureaux de change in banks, airports and the main station. Banks usually offer the best currency exchange rates. Most bureaux de change, travel agencies and hotels accept euro traveller's cheques for cashing.

Around 60 per cent of Leipzig's shops, restaurants, bars and hotels accept major credit cards, so it's worth checking before you pay. It's wise to carry a small amount of cash just in case.

HEALTH, SAFETY & CRIME

Leipzig is a safe city to visit and there are no particular health risks. No immunisations or health certificates are required and the tap water is safe to drink.

Medical care is of a high standard in Germany. Pharmacies (*Apotheken*) can treat minor ailments and usually open 09.00–18.00 Monday to Friday and 09.00–12.00 Saturday. Your hotel should be able to arrange for you to see an English-speaking doctor, if necessary. Pharmacies in Germany are symbolised by a red stylised 'A' on a white background.

EU citizens are entitled to free or reduced-cost emergency health care in Germany with a valid European Health Insurance Card (EHIC), which entitles you to state medical treatment but does not cover repatriation or long-term illness. There is a charge for routine medical care. All travellers should invest in a good health insurance policy before visiting.

The crime rate in Leipzig is low. While they are in a minority, members of the extreme right (neo-fascists) have been associated with violent outbursts towards those they consider 'foreign', so it's wise to keep your wits about you. If you are the victim of a crime, you should inform the police by calling ⓣ 110 (see *Emergencies*).

OPENING HOURS

Most shops open 09.00–20.00 Monday to Friday and

09.00–16.00 Saturday. Some open on Sundays in the tourist areas. Major shopping malls like the Hauptbahnhof stay open daily until 22.00.

TOILETS

Leipzig has a number of clean public toilets in the centre. Most are accessible for travellers with disabilities and offer baby-changing facilities. You'll need €0.50 to unlock the door at the city's 24-hour automatic toilets. If you need to freshen up on arrival, the shower at the main station costs around €7. Most restaurants, bars and large stores have facilities for customers; if you are only popping into, say, a bar to use their convenience, it is polite to buy a drink.

CHILDREN

There is plenty to keep tots and teens on their toes in Leipzig, from free play in the huge parks and gardens to boating Plagwitz's canals and riding horses through the Auenwald forest.

In the summer, take your kids to Lake Cospuden or Lake Kulkwitz to splash in clear waters, let off steam on the beach or go to the zoo. A 50 per cent reduction is usually offered for children, and kids are welcome in most restaurants and cafés. Drugstores in the city centre like DM and Müller stock everything from nappies to organic baby food. Most stores and public toilets have clean baby-changing facilities.

The **LVB group ticket** (Ⓦ www.lvb.de) is a real result for families. Covering up to five people, it offers great value for money on Leipzig's public transport network. Kids aged 6 to 13 years travelling alone get special discounts.

Fischer-Art's bright murals enliven the city

Belantis (ⓐ Zur Weissen Mark 1 ⓣ 1378 40 30 30
ⓦ www.belantis.de) is just south of Leipzig but is worth a trip
out. Kids love the rides, roller coasters and giant pirate ship at
this theme park and family tickets are available. The shamelessly
named **Euro Eddy's Family Fun Centre** (ⓐ Kastanienweg 1
ⓣ 0341 940 6244 ⓦ www.euroeddy-leipzig.de) is a huge indoor
adventure playground that keeps boredom at bay with its slides,
ball pits, bumper cars and climbing walls.

COMMUNICATIONS
Internet
Internet cafés have sprouted up all over the centre recently.
Expect to pay between €1.50 and €3 for an hour online. Some
cafés and bars with AOL terminals offer free, limited access for
customers, including 100 Wasser and Barfusz on Barfussgässchen,
and Bar Central on Nikolaistrasse. Other popular centres are:

Hamster Ecke ⓐ Gorkistrasse 129 ⓣ 0341 319 9022
ⓦ www.hamsterecke.de ⓛ 13.00–23.00 Mon–Fri

Intertelcafé ⓐ Brühl 64 ⓣ 0341 462 5879 ⓦ www.intertelcafe.de
ⓛ 10.00–22.00

Interphone ⓐ Cichoriusstrasse 2 ⓣ 0341 699 1717 ⓛ 10.00–22.00

Trixom ⓐ Härtelstrasse 21 ⓣ 0341 3559 0296 ⓦ www.trixom.de
ⓛ 11.00–02.00

Wireless internet access (Wi-Fi) has become widespread in
Leipzig, with a fair share of cafés, restaurants and bars offering it
on their menu – sometimes free for customers. Try:

Albert's Restaurant, Café & Bar ⓐ Markt 9

Bagel Brothers ⓐ Nikolaistrasse 42

Buddha Art Gallery ⓐ Neumarkt 9-19

CAM Café am Markt Bar ⓐ Katharinenstrasse 2
Leipzig-Halle Airport ⓐ Terminalring 11
Leipzig Hauptbahnhof ⓐ Willy-Brandt-Platz 5

Phone

Leipzig's modern public telephone boxes are glass with a grey and pink strip. Only a handful of these accept coins (minimum charge of €0.20), so you'll need to purchase a prepaid phone card from a newsagent, post office, station or T-Punkt store. These are available in denominations of €5, €10 and €20.

Alternatively, many of the city's internet cafés double up as call centres and offer good deals on international calls. Two useful numbers are:

National Directory Enquiries ☎ 11833, or 11837 for an English-speaking service

International Directory Enquiries ☎ 11834

Post

Stamps are sold in post offices and some newsagents. It costs around €0.70 to send a standard letter or postcard to Europe,

TELEPHONING GERMANY
To call Leipzig, dial 0049 for Germany, then 341 for Leipzig followed by the four- to seven-digit number.

TELEPHONING ABROAD
To call out of Germany, simply dial 00 followed by the country code and the local number.

and by airmail to North America, Australia, South Africa and New Zealand it is around €2. In addition to normal postal services, most post offices stock a good range of stationery, have ATMs and occasionally a bureau de change. The main **post office** (ⓦ www.deutschepost.de) in the city centre is on Augustusplatz.

ELECTRICITY

The electricity system in Germany is very reliable. It is 230 volts, 50 Hertz (round, two-pin plugs). Visitors from the UK and US will need adaptors.

TRAVELLERS WITH DISABILITIES

Leipzig caters to travellers with special needs. Most of the city's key attractions are wheelchair-friendly, featuring ramps, accessible toilets and low-level lift buttons. Among the best are the Old Town Hall, the Grassi Museum Complex, the Fine Arts Museum, Leipzig Museum, the Monument to the Battle of the Nations and Botanic Gardens. Many offer concessions (*Ermässigung*) for visitors with disabilities.

Good restaurant choices for travellers with disabilities include the Bachstüb'l, Auerbachs Keller, Bayerischer Bahnhof and the beer garden at Gosenschenke Ohne Bedenken.

Wheelchair-accessible toilets are located in Clara-Zetkin-Park, Augustusplatz, Karl-Liebknecht-Strasse and Goethestrasse.

Germany

NATKO (National Tourism Coordination Agency for All People e. V.)

ⓣ 0211 33 68 001 ⓦ www.natko.de

United Kingdom and Ireland
British Council of Disabled People (BCDP) ☎ 01332 295551
🌐 www.bcodp.org.uk

USA and Canada
Society for Accessible Travel & Hospitality (SATH) ☎ 212 447 7284
🌐 www.sath.org
Access-Able 🌐 www.access-able.com

Australia and New Zealand
Accessibility 🌐 www.accessibility.com.au
Disabled Persons Assembly ☎ 04 801 9100 🌐 www.dpa.org.nz

TOURIST INFORMATION

Dessau Tourist Information Book accommodation, tickets and guided city tours at Dessau's tourist office. 📍 Zerbster Strasse 2c ☎ 0340 204 1442 🌐 www.dessau.de 🕐 09.00–18.00 Mon–Fri, 09.00–13.00 Sat, Apr–Oct; 09.00–17.00 Mon–Fri, 10.00–13.00 Sat, Nov–Mar

German National Tourist Office Well-designed, this site is a mine of information. Brochures can be ordered online. 🌐 www.germany-tourism.de

Halle Stadmarketing Browse leaflets, pick up maps and book accommodation at Halle's helpful little visitor centre. 📍 Leipziger Strasse 105–106 ☎ 0345 122 9984 🌐 www.stadtmarketing-halle.de 🕐 09.00–19.00 Mon–Fri, 10.00–16.00 Sat, 10.00–14.00 Sun

Leipzig Erleben This visitor centre offers insightful themed tours of Leipzig and the surrounding area. 📍 Richard-Wagner-Strasse 1

📞 0341 710 4230 🌐 www.leipzig-erleben.com 🕐 10.00–18.00 Mon–Fri, 09.00–16.00 Sat, 10.00–14.00 Sun

Leipzig Tourist Service e.V. Leipzig's friendly and helpful tourist office provides information, maps, timetables, souvenirs and an accommodation and ticket booking service. 🅰 Richard-Wagner-Strasse 1 📞 0341 710 4265 🌐 www.leipzig.de 🕐 09.30–18.00 Mon–Fri (10.00–18.00 Nov–Feb), 09.30–16.00 Sat, 09.30–15.00 Sun

Saale Tourist This tourist office provides information on the Saale region, from art and culture to events and accommmodation. 🅰 Alter Markt 2, Halle 📞 0345 470 1480 🌐 www.saale-tourist.de 🕐 11.00–17.00 Tues–Fri, 11.00–16.00 Sat & Sun

Visit Saxony This comprehensive site gives an overview of Saxony and you can order brochures online. 📞 0351 491 700 🌐 www.saxonytourism.com

BACKGROUND READING

The Leipzig Campaign: 1813 – Napoleon and the 'Battle of the Nations' by F. Maude. A fascinating account of the most significant battle ever to have taken place on German soil.
Neo Rauch: Para by Werner Spies and Gary Tinterow. Excellent overview of the career so far of Leipzig's celebrity artist. The text is in German and English, but it's the illustrations that make this book essential.

Emergencies

The following are national free emergency numbers:
Police ⓘ 110
Fire & ambulance ⓘ 112
Breakdown (ADAC) ⓘ 0180 222 2222

When you dial the European emergency number 112, ask for the service you require and give details of where you are, what the emergency is and the number of the phone you are using. The operator will connect you to the service you need.

POLICE
Each of Germany's 16 states has its own police force (*Landespolizei*). The Federal Government police force is called the (*Bundespolizei*);

EMERGENCY PHRASES

Help!	**Fire!**	**Stop!**
Hilfe!	Feuer!	Halt!
Heelfe!	*Foyer!*	*Halt!*

Please call an ambulance/a doctor/the police/the fire service!
Rufen Sie bitte einen Krankenwagen/einen Arzt/
die Polizei/die Feuerwehr!
*Roofen zee bitter inen krankenvaagen/inen artst/
dee politsye/dee foyervair!*

---

it patrols at airports, train stations and country borders. Traditionally, police officers in Germany wear green uniforms, although this is gradually being phased out in favour of blue uniforms like most other EU police forces.

MEDICAL SERVICES

It is strongly recommended to have a valid health insurance policy before travelling to Germany. EU citizens are entitled to free or reduced-cost emergency health care with a European Health Insurance Card (EHIC). Pharmacies (*Apotheken*) are usually open 09.00–18.00 Monday to Friday and 09.00–12.00 Saturday. In case of accident or serious illness call ☎ 112

EMBASSIES

Australia Embassy ⓐ Wallstrasse 76–79, Berlin ☎ 030 700 129 129 ⓦ www.australian-embassy.de 🕐 09.00–11.00 Mon, Wed & Fri

Canada Embassy ⓐ Leipziger Platz 17, Berlin ☎ 030 203 120 ⓦ www.canada.de 🕐 08.00–12.30, 13.30–17.00 Mon–Fri

Republic of Ireland Embassy ⓐ Friedrichstrasse 200, Berlin ☎ 030 238 5174 ⓦ www.botschaft-irland.de 🕐 09.30–12.30, 14.30–16.45 Mon–Fri

South Africa Embassy ⓐ Tiergartenstrasse 18, Berlin ☎ 030 220 730 ⓦ www.suedafrika.org 🕐 09.00–12.00 Mon–Fri (lines are open for phone contact 14.00–16.30)

UK Embassy ⓐ Wilhelmstrasse 70–71, Berlin ☎ 030 204 570 ⓦ www.britischebotschaft.de 🕐 09.00–17.30 Mon–Fri

USA Embassy ⓐ Clayallee 170, Berlin ☎ 030 238 5174 ⓦ http://berlin.usembassy.gov 🕐 08.30–12.00 Mon–Fri

Editorial/project management: Lisa Plumridge
Copy editor: Paul Hines
Layout/DTP: Alison Rayner

The publishers would like to thank the following individuals and organisations for supplying their copyright photographs for this book: LTS/Schmidt, page 15; Andy Christiani, pages 19 & 132; Neil Setchfield, all others

The author would like to thank Andy Christiani for his help in preparing this book.

Send your thoughts to
books@thomascook.com

- Found a great bar, club, shop or must-see sight that we don't feature?
- Like to tip us off about any information that needs a little updating?
- Want to tell us what you love about this handy little guidebook and more importantly how we can make it even handier?

Then here's your chance to tell all! Send us ideas, discoveries and recommendations today and then look out for your valuable input in the next edition of this title.

Email the above address (stating the title) or write to:
CitySpots Series Editor, Thomas Cook Publishing, PO Box 227, Coningsby Road, Peterborough PE3 8SB, UK.